THE MONSTER BOOK OF MAGIC

MAGICIANS PLEASE READ!

This book is full of clever tricks to learn and perform to amaze
your friends, but remember to be very careful when using sharp
objects like knives or scissors, and when you put anything close to
your eyes. Make sure that you put away all sharp objects carefully
and if you are worried about anything while you are doing a trick,
stop and ask an adult for help (don't forget to ask them to swear
to secrecy). Sorry we can't be there to help you, but so long as
you take care you'll have lots of fun.

And to parents – please note that every care has been taken
in the compilation of this book to consider safety and prevent
accidents. However, the author and publisher cannot take
responsibility for accidental damage or injury. Please supervise
young children while they carry out any tricks involving scissors or
other tools.

THE MONSTER BOOK OF MAGIC

Robinson Children's Books

Robinson Publishing Ltd
7 Kensington Church Court
London W8 4SP

First published in the UK by Robinson Publishing Ltd 1998

A copy of the British Library Cataloguing in Publication data is available
from the British Library

ISBN 1–85487–489–6

Printed and bound in the UK

10 9 8 7 6 5 4 3 2

CONTENTS

INTRODUCTION

Welcome to the Monster Book of Magic, a book which aims to guide you step-by-step into the wonderful secretive world of magic and perhaps lead you to a hobby – or even a career! – as a master magician.

I have graded the tricks with either one, two or three rabbits to indicate how hard it is to do. The simple tricks have one rabbit, the toughest ones have three. However, I'm sure, if you start at the beginning and work your way through the book, mastering everything you'll have no problems with even the toughest tricks. You'll have a quite impressive repertoire!

The book begins with a chapter full of automatic magic tricks with which you will amaze yourself when you try them! Then, as you progress through the book, it slowly advances teaching you some simple secrets with which you can dazzle your family and friends, before moving on to the basics of sleight of hand to enable you to entertain in the classroom, in the playground, on holiday or at parties.

Finally the book shows you how you can put together a complete act using the tricks you have learnt and even how to stage your own spectacular magic show!

Also, don't ignore the tips that are scattered throughout this book – success as a magician comes from much more than just knowing how the tricks are done. You may find inspiration and ideas from the brief biographies of magicians which are featured. Knowing about the fascinating history of magic has helped many magicians to achieve greater success.

And finally, when you do put on your show please remember to drop me a line to invite me!

Anthony Owen

ONE IS FUN

ALL

This first chapter is full of lots of great magic that you can perform by yourself. Just by following through the easy step-by-step instructions with the necessary requirements (or, as magicians call them, "props"), you will be amazed and surprised at the results!

None of them requires any difficult sleight of hand or secret preparations, so when you have learned the instructions – and decided what you are going to say (magicians call everything they say during their performance "patter", and you will find some tips on this later in the book) – you can use these amazing tricks to amaze and amuse others too!

✪ THE FLOATING ✪ SAUSAGE

This is a classic of the magician's art. Forget sawing women in half and pulling rabbits from hats. Producing cocktail sausages out of mid-air and floating them is what people want to see!

Requirements:

ALL YOU NEED TO PERFORM THIS TRICK ARE YOUR TWO INDEX FINGERS. YEP, YOU DON'T EVEN NEED A SAUSAGE – YOU'RE GOING TO PRODUCE THAT BY MAGIC!

1 Touch the tips of your index fingers together and touch them to your nose (Fig. A).

2 Very slowly move your fingers forward away from your nose. Amazingly, if you look between your fingertips you will see a little sausage! When the sausage appears, stop moving your fingers forward. That's the amazing appearing sausage.

Now here's how to make it float . . .

Ⓐ

3 Very gently move the tips of your index fingers apart a little way. Be very careful that you don't drop the sausage! Incredibly, the little sausage remains suspended in mid-air without any visible means of support!

4 Bring your fingertips back together (don't leave the sausage floating for too long!) and bring your fingertips – and the sausage – back to your nose. You can now separate your hands, since the sausage has vanished back into thin air!

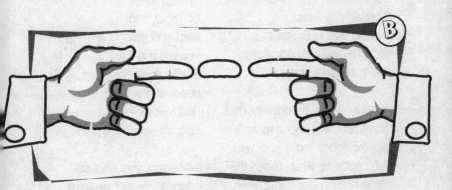

TOP TIPS FOR TRICKSTERS

Always practise what you are going to say with your tricks. This is known as the magician's patter and should be rehearsed as much as the working of the trick.

HYPNOTIZED ARM

This is a great trick to do on yourself, but you can also do it on your friends. The feeling is bizarre!

Requirements:

ALL THAT YOU NEED FOR THIS TRICK ARE AN OPEN DOORWAY AND YOUR TWO ARMS!

Stand in an open doorway, as though you are about to walk into the room. Move your arms out, until your wrists touch the inside of the door frame. Push your wrists hard against the frame and count slowly down from 30 to 1. Make sure that you are pushing outwards against the frame, almost as though you are trying to move the door frame. You really must push hard. If you do it correctly, and hard enough, you will feel the inside of your upper arm aching. Don't worry – the effect is worth the pain!

When you have finished counting to 30 (you must count very slowly), step out of the doorway and relax your arms. You will feel the strangest sensation – as though balloons are being blown up under your armpits and your arms will be pushed up. It's a very weeeeird feeling!

LINKING PAPERCLIPS

This is a great trick, in which you cause two household paper clips to leap magically off a piece of paper and then link together, apparently in mid-air!

Requirements:

YOU NEED A PIECE OF PAPER THAT IS ROUGHLY THE SIZE OF A BANKNOTE AND TWO REGULAR PAPERCLIPS. THEN PREPARE YOURSELF TO PARTICIPATE IN THIS GRAVITY-DEFYING MINI-ILLUSION!

Fold the paper twice into thirds to form the Z shape shown in Fig. 1. Insert the first

paperclip, at the point marked A, clipping together the front and centre folds of paper.

Insert the second paperclip at the point marked B, clipping together the back and centre folds. Both paperclips should now have their longer side facing towards you, as shown.

②

The piece of paper should now look like Fig. B. Hold the paper so that the clips are on the top edge and grab one of the short ends in each hand. Sharply pull the ends apart to unfold the note.

The paperclips will jump off the paper and into the air as though propelled by some mysterious magical force! And, even more amazingly, when they land the two separate clips are now linked together, just like the famous Chinese linking rings!

You can make this trick more spectacular by using real paper money or by using the giant coloured paperclips you can buy in stationery supply stores and a sheet of giant toy money. You could even attach coloured ribbons to the bottom of the paperclips, which will make the leaping paperclips look even more impressive.

TOP TIPS FOR TRICKSTERS

Always practise in front of a mirror or with a video camera so that you can see exactly how your tricks will look to your audience.

SUPER STARSIGN

In this trick a starsign is freely chosen and spelt out around the special star chart. Amazingly, your final landing place can be predicted, without knowing the starsign chosen.

Requirements:

FOR THIS YOU WILL NEED THE SPECIAL SUPER STARSIGN CHART (ILLUSTRATED).

First, try this out yourself.

1 Place your finger on any starsign on the chart. You have a completely free choice.

2 Starting on the next sign clockwise around the chart, spell out the name of your selected starsign, each starsign you encounter standing for one letter.

3 You have now landed on a new starsign. Repeat the spelling procedure as in

step 2 (remembering to start with the next sign for the first letter), but this time spell out the sign you have landed on.

4 When you have done this, you will have landed on yet another starsign. Alongside this sign is a number, which relates to the month that covers most of that starsign. Counting clockwise around the chart (again starting with the next sign), move that number of starsigns.

5 It may seem impossible for anyone to know where you have finally landed, but I do . . . you're on Sagittarius!

If you want to perform this trick on your friends, simply repeat these instructions to them and they will always end up on Sagittarius, too!

Before you begin the trick, you might want to seal inside an envelope a piece of paper that will be your "prediction".

Explain to your "audience" that this is what you think is going to happen in the future. Of course, on the piece of paper you have written: "You will land on Sagittarius!" When they have followed your instructions, you can open the envelope and prove that your prediction is completely correct!

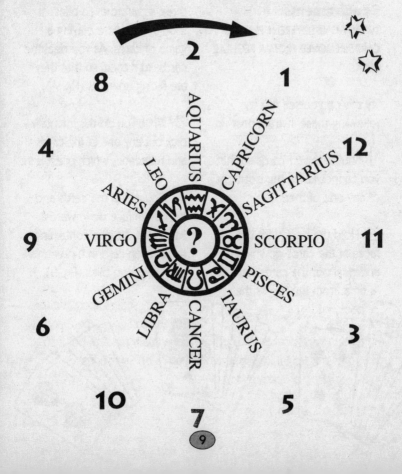

THE TWENTY-ONE CARD TRICK

In this simple – but impressive – card trick, you magically predict a playing card.

Requirements:

TWENTY-ONE DIFFERENT PLAYING CARDS REMOVED FROM A REGULAR DECK.

Try this on yourself first by following these instructions.

1 Shuffle the 21 cards so that you cannot know the positions of any one of them.

2 Hold the pack with the faces of the cards downwards and deal out the cards, one at a time, from the top of the pack, into three separate even piles, as though you were playing a game of cards. As you deal the cards, turn them so that they are facing upwards (Fig. A).

3 While you do this, mentally pick out any one of the cards and remember which pile it is in.

4 Square up the cards and turn them face downwards. Sandwich the pile containing the chosen card in between the other two piles (Fig. B).

10

5 Once again repeat the procedure in step 2. Deal out the same 21 cards into three piles, making sure that you notice which one now contains your chosen card, since it may have moved to one of the other two piles. Sandwich the pile containing your card in between the other two and turn them all face downwards.

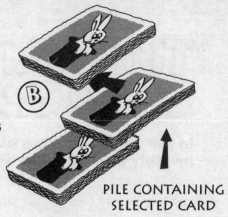

PILE CONTAINING
SELECTED CARD

6 One final time, repeat the dealing of the cards, remember the pile with your card and, again, sandwich it in between the other two.

7 Amazingly, if you've done everything right, at this point your card will always be 11 cards from the top of the pile (Fig. C).

When you want to perform this effect for somebody else, just ask them to tell you which pile contains their card each time.

To reveal their card at the end of the trick, deal the cards one at a time on to the table, turning them face up as you do so. When you get to the eleventh card, stop before you turn it face up and ask them to name their card. When they do, turn over the card and prove that you stopped at the right place!

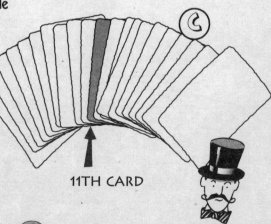

11TH CARD

THE PIANO CARD TRICK

In this classic effect, a playing card flies across invisibly from one pile to another.

Requirements:

ALL THAT YOU NEED FOR THIS ARE A PACK OF CARDS AND A PAIR OF HANDS.

Hold your hands as in Fig. A, so that your knuckles are touching the table top.

From the pack, remove a pair of playing cards, and place them into one of the spaces between your fingers, tucking

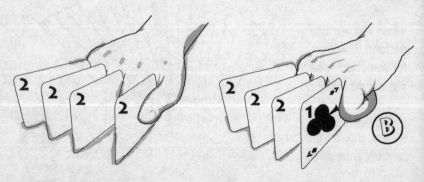

them into position.
Repeat this until you have a
pair of cards in each space
between your fingers – except
for one. Into this last space,
insert just one card. This is the
"odd card" (Fig. B).
Remove one pair of cards from
between your fingers and
separate them. Place each one
side by side on the table,
beginning two piles.

Remove all the remaining pairs,
separating them and adding
one card to each pile. When
you are down to just the last
"odd card", decide which pile
you will add it to. This pile will
now obviously contain an odd
number of cards.

However, amazing as it may
sound, that odd card has
actually jumped across invisibly
to what was the even pile. You
can prove it! Replace the
cards from the "odd" pile in
pairs between the fingers of
one hand, as you did at the
start. Incredibly, all the cards
will be paired up – the odd
card has vanished!
Replace what you thought was
the even pile in pairs between
the fingers of the other hand.
You will be left with one odd
card. It really did jump across!

If you perform this for your
friends, you can put the cards
in between their fingers and
ask them to select which pile
you should add the odd card
to. You can take the credit for
doing the magic, even
though you are
actually as
amazed as they
are!

13

THROUGH THE BLACK HOLE

You tie a knot in a piece of rope and push it through a tube. When the rope comes out the other end of the tube, the knot has vanished!

Requirements:

YOU WILL NEED A LENGTH OF ROPE OR STRING AND A SMALL TUBE. YOU COULD USE A MATCHBOX COVER OR EVEN A TOILET ROLL TUBE!

Drape the rope around the tube and tie a regular overhand knot around it, as in Fig. 1.

Push end A of the rope inside end X of the tube until it comes out of end Y. Slide the knot off of end X of the tube and push this into the tube, too.

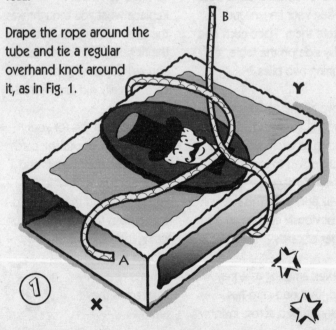

1

TRICKS YOU CAN BUY

Some tricks you may be able to buy from magic dealers or suppliers. You will find a short list of these at the end of this book or you may find some listed in your local yellow pages.

1. COIN UNIQUE – *This is a very effective set of fake coins with which you can make a coin vanish under impossible conditions.*

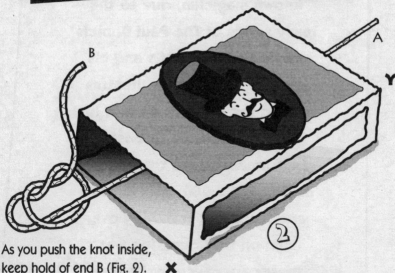

As you push the knot inside, keep hold of end B (Fig. 2). ✖

Pull end A until the rope has been pulled right through the tube. Now the knot that went inside the tube has completely disappeared!

You can perform this for others by explaining that the tube is a special "black hole" and that, although the rope survives, the knot gets sucked away and vanishes forever.

PAUL DANIELS

1938 –

Paul Daniels is Britain's best
known magician, due to the
many series of The Paul Daniels
Magic Show on BBC1 and his
live performances in theatres
around the country. One of his
most memorable television
performances was the day he
made £1,000,000 cash vanish –
and reappear! Watching over
him on that occasion was
newspaper tycoon, Robert
Maxwell!

A HOLE IN YOUR HAND

Did you know that you can see right through the middle of your hand? You can with this trick!

Requirements:

ANY SMALL TUBE. IT CAN BE THE INSIDE OF A KITCHEN OR TOILET ROLL OR JUST A ROLLED-UP PIECE OF PAPER.

With your right hand, hold the tube to your right eye. Place your left hand over your left eye with your palm facing towards your eye and the edge of your hand against the tube (see illustration). It is important that you keep both eyes open.

Now slowly move your left hand away from your eye, but make sure that the edge keeps touching the tube. When your left hand is about 4 inches (10 cm) away from your left eye, it should appear as if the tube is actually passing right through your left hand – and you can still see right through it! When you have exactly the correct position, it looks amazing!

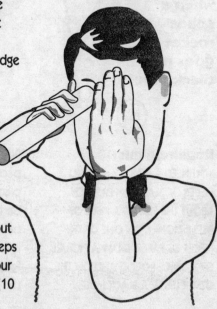

THE SPACE ROCKET AND THE BLACK HOLE

Using two
pieces of
paper, a
pencil –
and some
magic –
you can
show what
happens
when a
space
rocket
goes near a
black hole!

Ⓐ

Requirements:

YOU NEED A PENCIL AND TWO PIECES OF BLANK PAPER, EACH ABOUT THE SIZE OF A PIECE OF PAPER MONEY. ON ONE OF THE PIECES OF PAPER, DRAW A PICTURE OF A SPACE ROCKET AND ON THE OTHER DRAW A BLACK HOLE.

Place the black hole piece of paper on a flat surface and place the space rocket piece on top so that the pieces of paper form a T-shape (Fig. A). It is important that the rocket forms the horizontal line and the black hole the vertical line.

Place the pencil horizontally along the top edge of the space rocket drawing and roll it downwards. Roll both of the pieces of paper around the pencil (Fig. B). Continue rolling until you have reached the bottom of the T and both pieces of paper are completely wrapped around the pencil.

Now slowly roll the pencil back the other way, unrolling both pieces of paper as you go. When you have unrolled both pieces you will be amazed to discover that the pieces of paper have actually changed places! The rocket ship drawing, which was on top of the black hole drawing, is now underneath it. Incredibly the rocket ship got sucked right through the black hole!

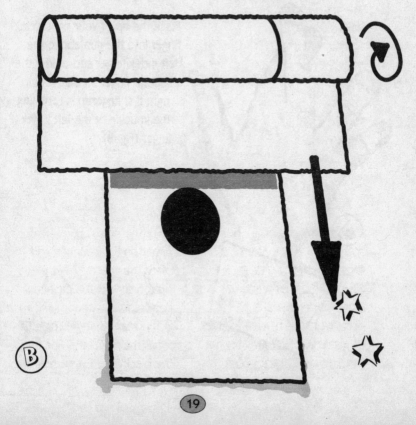

THE EXTRA LONG FINGER

With this trick, you can stretch your index finger to almost twice its original length!

Requirements:
YOUR TWO HANDS!

Bend your left index finger

below your left second finger (Fig. A) so that the tip emerges from the left side of your second finger.

Place the tip of your right index finger into the gap above the left index finger and below the second finger so that your right first fingertip is touching the knuckle of the left index finger (Fig. B).

With your hands in this position, it looks as if the tip of your left index finger is actually the tip of your right index finger, which has been stretched to twice its length. It really does look weird!

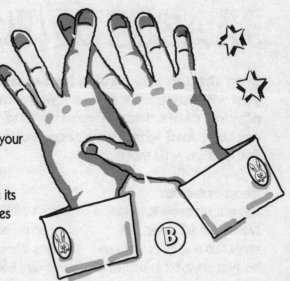

ELEVEN FINGERS?

This will teach you how to count your fingers to prove that you have eleven!

Requirements:

YOUR TWO HANDS AGAIN.

Hold up your left hand in a fist. Straighten out your left thumb and say, "Ten." Straighten out your left indexfinger and say, "Nine." Straighten out your left second finger and say, "Eight."

Straighten out your left third finger and say, "Seven."

Straighten out your left little finger and say, "Six."

Open your right hand and say, "Five here. And five plus six equals eleven!" – That's it!

MAGIC SQUARE

Even though you have a free choice of where you will move in a magic square of nine playing cards, I know exactly where you will end up. And when you show your family and friends so will you!

Requirements:

YOU WILL NEED NINE PLAYING CARDS – THE ACE, THREE, FIVE, SEVEN AND NINE OF HEARTS AND THE TWO, FOUR, SIX AND EIGHT OF SPADES.

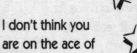

Lay out the nine cards in a 3 by 3 grid – or magic square – in numerical order as illustrated.

Follow the instructions below. When I ask you to move, you can move to the card above or below or to the left or right of the card you are touching – but not diagonally.

Choose any one of the red cards as your starting point. The choice is yours.

Move three times.

I don't think you are on the ace of hearts. Remove that card from the grid.

Move three more times.

I don't think you are on the two or four of spades. Remove both those cards.

Move five times.

I don't think you are on the three or seven of hearts. Remove both those cards.

Move twice.

I don't think you are on the nine of hearts. Remove that card.

Move once.

You are on the five of hearts!

If you want to perform this for your family and friends, write

these instructions on a piece of card and give this to them. If you make sure that they follow the instructions exactly – remember: no diagonal moves! – it will always work for you, too!

MELTING MONEY

You can make a coin vanish beneath a glass of water!

Requirements:

A CLEAR GLASS TUMBLER FILLED WITH WATER, A COIN AND AN OPAQUE SAUCER.

Place the coin on a flat surface and place the glass of water on top so that you can see the coin through the bottom of the glass.

Cover the mouth of the glass with the saucer. Now when you look into the glass tumbler through the sides you will be unable to see the coin below the base! The coin has completely vanished.

As you read through this book, you will learn ways by which you can produce a duplicate (identical) coin to amaze your friends even more!

T. NELSON DOWNS
(1867 – 1938)

T. Nelson Downs was an American magician who billed himself as the 'King of Koins' (sic). As a railway clerk he spent his spare time learning sleight of hand with coins and creating his own variations. He turned professional and almost overnight became a big vaudeville star with his unique and original act of apparently producing coins from mid-air. One of his most challenging moves is the 'Downs Coin Star' in which coins balanced on the tips of the four fingers and thumb vanish and re-appear.

CHUNG LING SOO
(1861 – 1918)

One of the highlights of Chung Ling Soo's flamboyant, spectacular full evening show was the 'Dream of Wealth'. From mid-air he produced coins, banknotes and a cheque for one million pounds! Although known as the Marvellous Chinese Conjurer the oriental character was a disguise for William E. Robinson who was actually born in America! He died after being shot on stage during his performance of the famous 'Catching a Bullet'.

KNOT PUZZLE

How can you tie a knot in a piece of rope without letting go of either end? It can be done, when you know the secret!

Requirements:

A LENGTH OF ROPE, AT LEAST 18 INCHES (45 CM) LONG.

Place the rope on a table in front of you. Fold your arms – this is the sneaky secret! Now pick up the right end of the rope in your left hand and the left end of the rope in your right hand (see illustration).

Hold tight on to the ends and slowly unfold your arms. You will see the "knot" that you made with your arms actually being transferred into the rope as you unfold your arms. It looks really magical!

When your arms are unfolded, you will see that, without letting go of either end of the rope, there is now a knot in its middle!

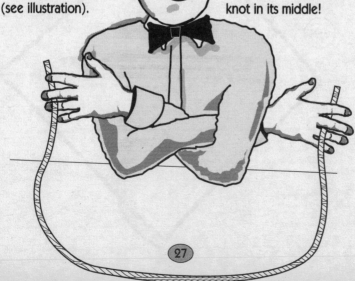

PENCIL THROUGH HANDKERCHIEF

A solid pencil passes right through a solid handkerchief!

Requirements:
A LARGE, CLEAN HANDKERCHIEF AND A PENCIL.

Lay out the handkerchief flat on the table in a diamond shape. One corner should point towards you, one should point away from you and the two diagonally opposite corners should be parallel with your shoulders.

Imagine that there is a line running across the middle of the handkerchief connecting the

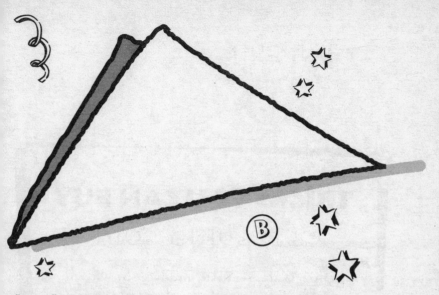

diagonally opposite corners. Place the pencil on top of the handkerchief so that it is slightly above, and parallel with, that imaginary line (Fig. A).

Fold the bottom half of the handkerchief away from you, along the imaginary line, so that the corner formerly at the bottom and pointing towards you ends up slightly above the top corner (Fig. B).

Through the folds of the handkerchief, roll the pencil away from you. As you roll, the handkerchief will wrap itself around the pencil. Do not roll completely to the upper corner. Before you reach this point, the lower corner will pop out towards you from beneath the pencil. Hold this corner with your right hand. Place your left index finger on the upper corner to hold it place. With your right hand, pull the corner you are holding towards you.

Once the handkerchief is completely unrolled, remove it to reveal that the pencil is now underneath – it has magically passed through the handerchief completely unharmed

TRICKS YOU CAN BUY

2. FOLDING COIN

This is a specially made coin which will enable you to push a large coin inside a bottle and do many other impressive tricks.

FOOL THE FAMILY AND DAZZLE YOUR FRIENDS!

This chapter is full of stunts and tricks that you can use to fool and amaze your family and friends. Most of them have a special secret that – like all good magicians – you should never reveal. If you do, you will spoil the surprise and fun – and, most importantly, you will look less impressive!

THAT'S TORN IT!

This puzzle will beat your friends every time. It may seem to be a very simple challenge to tear a piece of pre-cut paper into three sections, but however many times they try, your friends will be unable to do it. You will eventually reveal the simple solution.

Requirements:

YOU WILL NEED A PIECE OF PAPER WITH TWO SLITS CUT IN IT (FIG. A). MAKE SURE THAT YOU DO NOT CUT RIGHT TO THE OPPOSITE EDGE.

Challenge someone to hold the paper with a short end in each hand. Tell them to pull it into three separate strips. They will always be left with two pieces – a single section and a double section. Try it yourself and you will find it is impossible to tear it into three.

However, there is a simple solution that you can reveal when everybody is suitably fed up! Before you pull on the ends, hold the top edge of the middle section in your mouth (Fig. B). Then pull – you will be left with three separate pieces!

32

REFLEX TESTER

This is a "scam" you can use to prove to your friends that there is no such thing as "easy money". If you use their money, perhaps you can make a profit!

Requirements:
ANY PIECE OF PAPER MONEY.

Hold the note by gripping the middle of the right long edge with your right thumb and index finger. Hold your open left hand in position at the middle of the left long edge. It is important that the left hand does not actually touch the money.

Your right hand releases the money and your left hand instantly closes to catch it. You might want to repeat this a few times to show how easy it is.

Now ask your friend to hold their open left hand at the centre point of the left long side, taking the place of your left hand.

Tell your friend that if they catch the money they can keep it! This is very funny if you have borrowed the money from somebody else!

Open your right fingers to release the money and watch it slip through your friend's fingers to the floor. Although this looks easy, nobody will be fast enough to catch the money.

TORN WALLPAPER

This is more of a cruel practical joke than a trick – but it is great fun!

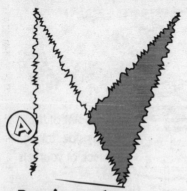

(A)

that the fold is at the bottom edge parallel with the floor. It will appear as if your friend's wallpaper has been ripped! Just watch their reaction when they come back into the room!

One final point: make sure that you use one of the many non-permanent adhesives to attach the piece of paper to the wallpaper. Don't use glue!

Requirements:

ALL YOU NEED IS A PIECE OF BLANK WHITE PAPER, A NON-PERMANENT ADHESIVE AND A FRIEND WITH WALLPAPER AND A GOOD SENSE OF FUN.

While you are alone in a room in your friend's home, fold the piece of white paper and tear the sides so that they are ragged as shown in Fig. A. Using the non-permanent adhesive, attach the paper to the wallpaper as in Fig. B, so

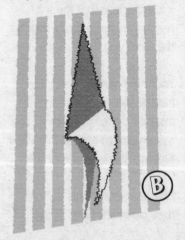

(B)

FRED KAPS
(1926 - 1980)

This Dutch magician was a master
of sleight of hand and
manipulation. He was a winner of
the famous F.I.S.M. Grand Prix,
making him a true World Champion.
His act featured the manipulation
of banknotes and giant coins and
concluded with the production of
an almost endless stream of salt
pouring from his fist.

WIGGLE YOUR FINGER

This is a great "body magic" stunt that you can do any time. It's always good to know a few tricks that, at the drop of a hat, you can do with your fingers and hands. (The Floating Sausage and The Extra Long Finger in the first chapter are good examples.)

Requirements:

A FLAT SURFACE AND A FRIEND
WITH A HAND!

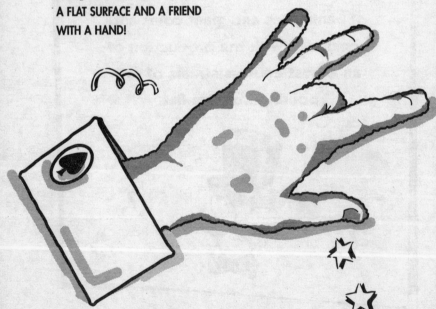

Ask your friend to place their hand on a flat surface, with the tip of their second finger bent into their palm so that the knuckle of this finger touches the surface, while all the other fingers and the thumb are spread out with their tips touching the surface (see illustration).

Surprisingly, in this position it is impossible for anybody to wiggle their third finger. Try it yourself – it is amazing!

With this knowledge, you can make all kinds of cruel bets with your friends. You could bet them any amount that they can't wiggle all their fingers. You could even get them to place some money under their hand and tell them you will give them double if they can lift all their fingers off the tabletop whilst keeping their knuckle on it. They can't, so you get to keep the money!

What other scams can you come up with using this idea?

TOP TIPS FOR TRICKSTERS

Never repeat a trick for the same audience. The suprise is lost the second time and they will watch more closely!

SCRATCH OUT A PROFIT

This challenge with coins and a tumbler seems impossible, but when you know the special secret, it's easy!

Requirements:

A TABLE COVERED WITH TABLECLOTH, TWO SMALL COINS, ONE LARGE COIN AND A CLEAR GLASS TUMBLER.

Place the large coin flat on the table in between the two smaller ones. Turn the glass upside down and place it so that the rim is balanced on the two smaller coins and the large coin is isolated (Fig. A).

Tell your friends that, if they can remove the large coin from under the glass, they can keep it! However, they must remove it without touching the glass or either of the two smaller coins!

The secret is to scratch at the tablecloth alongside the glass (Fig. B). This will cause the large coin to creep very slowly out from underneath the glass into your waiting hand!

By the way, there is a way to get the large coin out that can be done on any flat surface and doesn't require a tablecloth. Can you work it out?

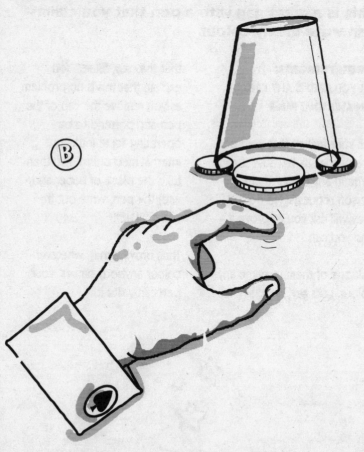

THE PEN THAT WRITES ANY COLOUR

This is a great gag with a pen that you claim can write in any colour.

Requirements:

ALL YOU NEED IS ANY KIND OF PEN AND SOME PAPER.

Tell your friends that your pen is very special, because it can write in any colour that a person requests. No doubt they will ask you to prove it – and you can.

Ask one of them to name any colour. Let's say, for example,

that they say, "Blue." You explain that this is no problem as you remove the cap of the pen and pretend to be operating some intricate internal mechanism. You then take the piece of paper and, with the pen, write out the *word* "BLUE"!

Thus proving that, whatever colour anybody names, your pen can write it!

FIND THE LADY

This is a variation of the famous Three Card Trick or Monte, often known as Find the Lady. This special version enables you to baffle and amaze your friends since, at the end, the queen completely vanishes!

Requirements:

YOU WILL NEED FOUR PLAYING CARDS FROM AN OLD PACK – ONE QUEEN AND THREE REGULAR CARDS. CUT OFF ONE LONG EDGE OF THE QUEEN AND TAPE THE BACK OF IT TO THE FACE OF ONE OF THE REGULAR CARDS, TO MAKE A FLAP

(FIG. A). THIS IS KNOWN AS A "FAKE" CARD.

Secret preparation: Set up the cards in a fan, with the fake card at the bottom. Insert one of the regular cards under the queen flap (Fig. B.) Place the

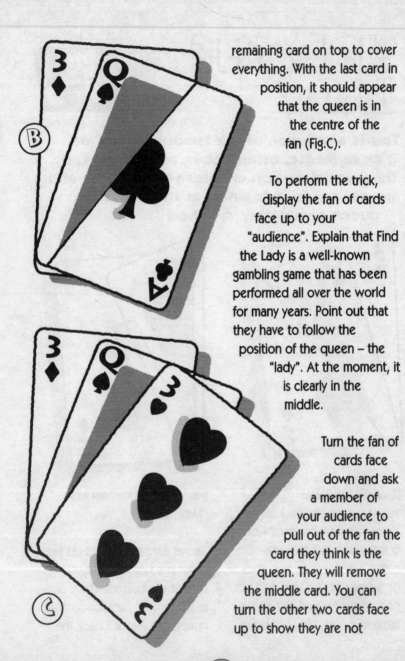

remaining card on top to cover everything. With the last card in position, it should appear that the queen is in the centre of the fan (Fig.C).

To perform the trick, display the fan of cards face up to your "audience". Explain that Find the Lady is a well-known gambling game that has been performed all over the world for many years. Point out that they have to follow the position of the queen – the "lady". At the moment, it is clearly in the middle.

Turn the fan of cards face down and ask a member of your audience to pull out of the fan the card they think is the queen. They will remove the middle card. You can turn the other two cards face up to show they are not queens, as long as you are careful not to reveal the flap (use the upper card of the two to cover it).

When your friend turns over the card that they believe is the queen, they will be amazed to discover that it has changed! You could write a surprise message on the face of this card, such as "You owe me a fortune!" or "I hope this has taught you never to gamble!"

HOW MUCH?

This is a great magic trick you can do to win money from your family and friends!

(A)

Requirements:

A TABLE ON WHICH TO PERFORM THE TRICK, ANY COIN AND SOME NON-PERMANENT ADHESIVE OR WAX.

Secret preparation: Before your "audience" arrives, secretly stick your coin underneath the table you are going to perform

on (Fig. A). Make sure that the coin is near to one of the edges and that you can easily remove the coin with the fingers of one hand.

Gather your family and friends around the table top and ask each of them to place one coin on the table. Explain that they have to remember the exact total of the coins to get their money back. It seems like a simple challenge.

When they have all added up the coins, use one hand to slide the coins into your other hand which is open and empty at the edge of the table. However, as the coins drop into your hand, your fingers secretly peel away the coin that you had stuck under the table beforehand (Fig. B). Add this to the coins in your hand!

When you ask your audience to guess the total, they will all announce the same amount. Then you announce your guess, adding on the value of the extra secret coin to the total of the coins on the table.

It is important that you announce your total after everybody else; otherwise someone might decide to copy your answer and demand to split your winnings!

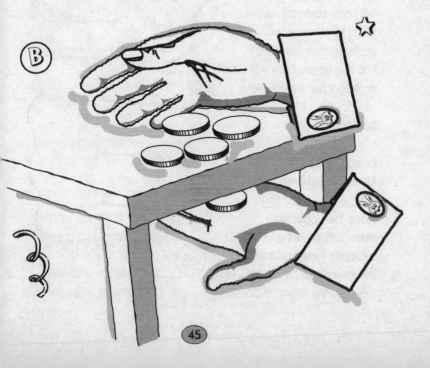

FISTS OF FUN

Using just one finger, you can separate your friend's fists, but even when you tell them the secret, they cannot separate yours!

Requirements:

JUST YOUR HANDS.

Ask one of your friends to form their hands into fists and place one on top of the other (Fig. A).

Tell them that you are going to attempt to separate their fists using just one finger. They will probably not believe you can do it.
But you can . . .

Extend your right index finger and, swinging your right arm, use the finger to strike the upper fist sharply. This will be sufficient to knock it off the lower one.

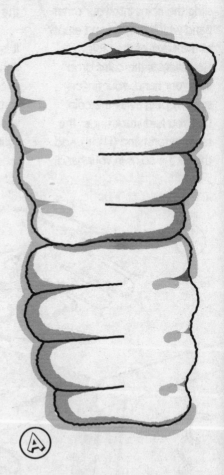

(A)

Now that they have seen how it can done, ask your friends if they would like to try it on you. No doubt they will! However, it doesn't matter how hard they whack their finger against your fist – they won't be able to budge it. Why?

Because you have secretly extended the thumb of the lower fist and are gripping it with the fingers of the upper fist (Fig. B)! In this position, they will never be able to separate your fists!

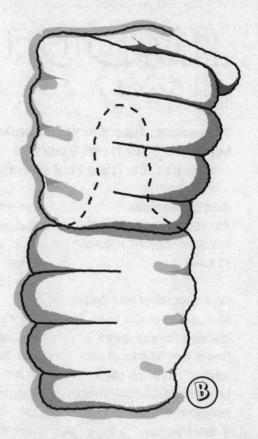

TRICKS YOU CAN BUY

3. CIGARETTE THROUGH COIN

As its name sugests this is a special coin through which you can push a borrowed cigarette.

HAND ON HEAD

This seems like a simple challenge – to separate your hand from the top of your head – but, in fact, it's a real toughie!

Requirements:

JUST YOU AND SOME FRIENDS WHOSE REPUTATIONS YOU WANT TO RUIN!

Place the palm of your right hand on top of your head. The challenge for your friends is simple: they have to lift your hand off of the top of your head (see illustration). They are not allowed to jerk it; they have to lift it.

This sounds easy to do, but as long as you concentrate and press down really hard on the top of your head, your friends will find it almost impossible to separate your hand from your head.

There's no special secret – just concentrate and press hard and they won't be able to do it! But you'll have great fun watching them struggle as they try!

TELEKINETIC BALL

The magician places a ball in the middle of the table and asks the audience to stand around the table and hold hands! As the audience concentrates, the ball mysteriously rolls across the table, apparently controlled by their thoughts. At the end, the audience can examine the ball – proof that it was a genuine psychic experience!

Requirements:

A TABLE WITH A TABLECLOTH, 3 FEET (1 M) OF THREAD, A RING AND A LIGHTWEIGHT BALL (E.G. A PING PONG BALL).

Secret preparation: Tie the ring to one end of the thread (see illustration on next page).

Before the audience comes into the room, place the ring flat in the centre of the table – under the tablecloth. Ensure that the thread is stretched out and dangles over the edge of the table where you can easily and inconspicuously grab hold of it.

To perform the trick, hand over the ball for examination. Explain that it is a mysterious kinetic crystal full of psychic powers. This should make your audience smile; some might even argue that it looks just like a ping pong ball.

When it has been checked by everybody and has "picked up the psychic vibrations from everybody in the room", take the ball back and rest it on the table. Make sure that it is inside the ring concealed underneath the tablecloth.

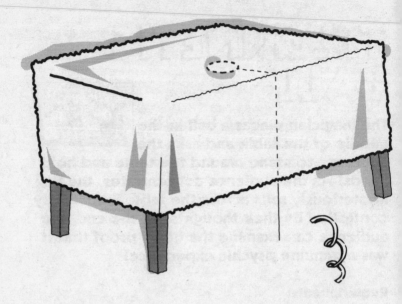

Invite your audience to join you around the table. As they move to the table, secretly take hold of the loose end of the thread. It is important that you do not pull it yet! Also, be careful that the thread does not get broken; otherwise you'll have to rely on real psychic power!

Ask your audience to stand around the table and hold hands. Standing outside of the circle, ask them to stare at the "crystal" and concentrate. Tell

them that they must say over and over to themselves in their minds: "Move, move, move." Don't be in a rush to make the ball move; allow the tension to build. You could even dim the lights slightly for this effect, and to make it even spookier!

When you feel the moment is right very gently pull on the thread – just a fraction – and then pause. The ball on the table will move slightly. Some people will think they saw the ball move. Some may have missed it. Some won't be sure if it moved or not, but they'll all be intrigued!

Pull the thread a bit more. The ball will move across the table top as the ring slides under the tablecloth and drags the ball with it.

Finally, ask someone to pick up the ball to examine it again. As they do, pull the thread and ring out from under the tablecloth and let them fall unnoticed on to the floor.

Get on the phone to Ghostbusters!

TOP TIPS FOR TRICKSTERS

Don't be afraid to ask members of the audience for constructive criticism after one of your performances. Listening to their comments and thinking about them will make you into a better magician.

PAPER CHASE

This is a fun challenge. You show your friends a sheet of newspaper. Explain that one of them will stand on one end of the newspaper and you will put a piece of paper money on the newspaper, too. If they can pick up the money, they get to keep it! If they can't pick it up, they have to give you money of equal value. This sounds like a good way to lose money, but you will win every time.

Requirements:

A SHEET OF NEWSPAPER, A PIECE OF PAPER MONEY AND A DOORWAY.

The doorway is the secret to this challenge. When somebody accepts your challenge, you place the sheet of newspaper in the doorway so that, when the door is closed, the newspaper will be trapped beneath – half of it on one side, half on the other side.

Place the money on the newspaper on one side of the door, close it and have your friend stand on the paper on the other side. Make sure that your friend – who by this time is probably an ex-friend! – stands on the side of the newspaper over which the door opens inwards, so that he cannot just open the door outwards and pick up the money! This way, if he tries to open the door he will be knocked off the newspaper.

Also don't do this with a stable door. Your friend will just open the top section and pick up the money!

AL GOSHMAN

New York magician, Al Goshman was
one of the first and finest close-up
magicians. Until his recent death he
was one of the resident magicians at
the Magic Castle in Hollywood.
Throughout his act, if you said
'please', he would produce a coin
from underneath a salt cellar – each
coin bigger than the last.

MOVING MATCHES

You lay out a row of matches on a table. While your back is turned your friends move as many matches around as they wish. Amazingly, immediately after turning back, you can tell them exactly how many matches were moved.

Requirements:
A BOX OF MATCHES.

As you lay out ten or so matches in a straight row on the table look out for one match that has a distinguishing mark, something that makes it different from all the rest – a small nick, lump or splinter. Casually arrange the matches so that this match goes at the far right end of the row (Fig. A). Do not draw attention to this match as it is going to be your "secret helper" in this stunt. Explain that, while your back is turned, you would like

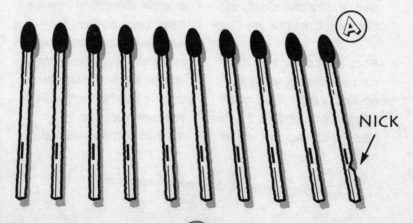

(A)

NICK

someone to move matches, one at a time, from the right end to the left end of the row. They can move as many or as few matches as they wish, but they must move them one at a time.

Turn your back and tell them to move the matches silently so that you cannot hear any clues!

When you turn back, all that you have to do is note the position of the marked match. Count to its position in the row from the left end; that will tell

you how many matches were moved. For example, if it is now in the fifth position, you know that five matches were moved (Fig. B).

If you wish, you could repeat the trick by deducting the match's first position (in the example above, five) from the match's new position. For example, if the second time the match was at position seven, and the first time you know that five matches were moved, you know (because 7 − 5 = 2) that two matches were moved.

TELEPHONE MIND-READING

This is a fun stunt to do when you are speaking to a friend on the telephone.

incredible psychic powers, you are going to be able to tell them exactly what they are holding in their hand. They probably won't believe you, but you can.

After a suitable build-up, tell them that they are holding – a telephone handset!

Requirements:
A FRIEND WITH A TELEPHONE.

When you are on the telephone to a friend, tell them that you can read their mind. No doubt they will ask you to prove it!

Tell them to pick up any object nearby and concentrate on it. Explain that, by using your

Remember, you didn't tell them which hand you were concentrating on! It's probably best to hang up before they get angry!

TELEPHONE MIND-READING II

This is another great telephone mind-reading trick – but this one really works! A friend on the other end of the telephone is able to name anybody's selected card!

Requirements:

A PACK OF CARDS AND A FRIEND WITH A TELEPHONE.

Secret preparations: You will need to arrange for your friend to be at home and to know the special secret code. When you say "Hello", he is to start counting: ace, two, three, four, five, six, seven, eight, nine, ten, jack, queen and king. When you interrupt him and say "Hello" again, he is to recite the names of the suits: "Clubs, hearts, spades, diamonds." This is the secret code.

When you know your friend is at home, ask somebody to select a playing card from a pack. Explain that it does not matter if you see what the card is as it is your friend who will be doing the trick!

When you know what the card is, call your friend. You will then secretly tell him the name of the card by interrupting him as he lists the numbers and

HELLO

suits. For example, say the card chosen was the five of spades. When your friend starts counting, interrupt him by saying "Hello" when he says "Five." As arranged, he will now start reciting the suits; when he says "Spades," interrupt him by saying something like, "Will you tell my friend which card they chose?"

You have secretly coded the selected card to your friend without anybody else knowing! You now pass the handset over to the selector of the card so that your friend can tell them its name!

Ace . . . two . . . three . . . four . . . five . . . SIX

6

THE NEXT CARD
I TURN OVER...

This is a classic "sucker" trick with a pack of cards. In sucker tricks, you make the audience think you have messed up, but at the end your magic wins through!

Requirements:

A REGULAR PACK OF PLAYING CARDS.

Secret preparation: Before you begin, hold the pack face down (so that the back design is on the top) and look at – and remember – the card on the bottom (face) of the pack. For the purpose of this explanation, let's assume it is the ace of diamonds.

Fan or spread the cards face down and ask a friend to remove any card. Tell them to show everybody the card (except you) and to remember it! It is important that you do not see the card. Square up the rest of the cards and ask your friend to place their card on top of the pack. Now ask them to split the pack in half and to place the bottom half of the pack on top so that their card is lost somewhere in the middle of the pack. They have to agree that there is no way you could know where the card is.

In fact, you know exactly where the card is! Because they replaced the bottom half of the pack on top of their card, this has placed their card right next to the card you looked at beforehand! To reveal their card, you could just deal the cards one at a time face up from the pack (held face down), looking for your remembered card (the ace of diamonds) and know that the next card was the chosen one.

However, I think it is more fun to do it this way: Deal through the pack as above, but continue dealing past the card you know was selected. The audience will think that you have messed up, but after a while, stop and say, "I bet the next card I turn over will be your card." As they have already seen you deal past their card, it is highly likely that they will bet with you. When you have shaken hands on the bet, reach into the pile of face-up cards you have already dealt, find the card you know to be their selection and turn it face down!

JUST CHANCE

This is a classic magic trick in which you offer members of your audience a chance to win some money. However, in the end, you always keep it!

Requirements:

FOUR ENVELOPES, ONE PIECE OF PAPER MONEY, A NON-PERMANENT ADHESIVE AND A TRAY.

Secret preparation: Like "How Much?" earlier in this chapter, this trick relies on secret preparation before you see your audience – and like "How Much?" it relies on sticking

money under something! This time it is a piece of paper money. Fold the money three times (Fig A1,2 and 3), and attach it to the underside of the tray (Fig. B). Stick it in a position so that it is covered by your fingers when they are gripping the edge of the tray.

Seal the four envelopes and place them in a row on top of

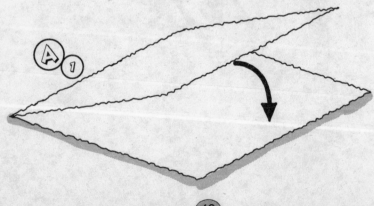

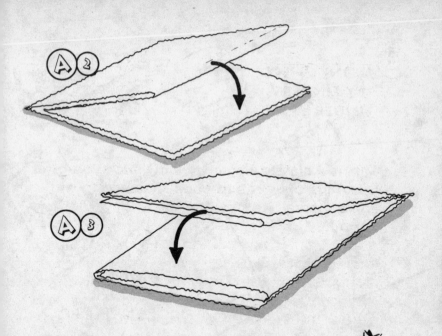

the tray. You are now set to perform Just Chance.

Ask three people to assist you explaining they could win some money. You should have no problem getting helpers for this trick!

Display the tray and explain that one of these four envelopes contains a folded-up piece of paper money. Ask the three assistants to each select an envelope from the tray, leaving one envelope on the tray. Explain that this is the envelope left for you. Clip this envelope under your thumb

STICK MONEY UNDER
TRAY HERE

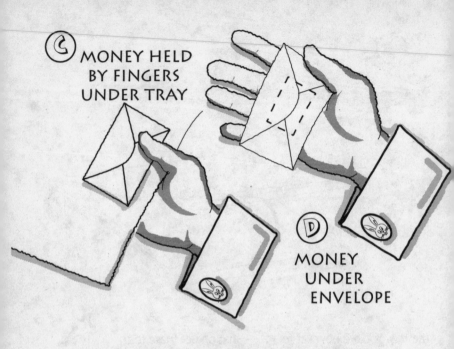

C MONEY HELD BY FINGERS UNDER TRAY

D MONEY UNDER ENVELOPE

(Fig. C) so that it is directly over the money on the underside of the tray.

Ask your three assistants to open their envelopes and remove the contents. While they are doing this, slide out the tray from your hand, so that your fingers release the money and keep it hidden behind your envelope (Fig. D). Get rid of the tray.

By this time, all three of your assistants should have opened their envelopes and found no money. Tear the top of your envelope and turn it upside down, apparently to tip out the contents. In fact, you release the money that you have been holding against the back of the envelope. If done correctly, it appears as though this money has come from inside the envelope. Pocket your winnings and commiserate with the three losers!

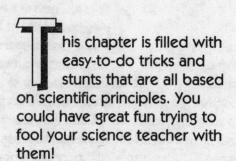

SCIENTIFIC WONDERS

This chapter is filled with easy-to-do tricks and stunts that are all based on scientific principles. You could have great fun trying to fool your science teacher with them!

FISHING FOR ICE

You challenge your friends to lift an ice cube out of a glass of water, without touching it and using just a length of string.

Requirements:

YOU WILL NEED A GLASS OF WATER, AN ICE CUBE, A LENGTH OF THIN STRING AND SOME TABLE SALT.

The solution is simple – it is the salt! Place the ice cube in the glass of water (Fig. A). Dangle the string in the glass so that the end rests on the ice cube. Sprinkle some salt on the cube, making sure you get plenty on the end of the string, too. Wait for about 30 seconds and then very gently pull up the string. You will discover that the cube is stuck to the end of it (Fig. B)! You have managed to get the ice cube out of the water without touching it!

LIQUID ILLUSION

This one is a bit more daring. Try it out over a sink first!

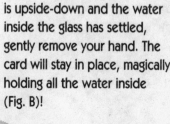

Requirements:

A GLASS APPROXIMATELY HALF FULL OF WATER AND A PIECE OF CARD BIG ENOUGH TO COVER THE MOUTH OF THE GLASS.

Place the card over the mouth of the glass (Fig. A). Place a hand flat on top of the card and slowly turn the glass upside-down, holding the card tightly in position throughout this operation. When the glass is upside-down and the water inside the glass has settled, gently remove your hand. The card will stay in place, magically holding all the water inside (Fig. B)!

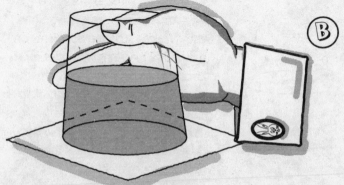

SALT AND PEPPER SEPARATION

Magically you are able to separate grains of salt and pepper.

Requirements:
SALT, PEPPER AND A COMB.

Mix a small amount of salt and pepper together in a pile on a clean, dry surface. To separate the salt and pepper, you use the comb!

Comb your hair with the comb. This builds up static electricity in the comb. Hold the comb about 3/4 inch (2 cm) over the pile of mixed salt and pepper. The static electricity will attract the pepper and cause it to leap up and stick to the comb! Knock the pepper off of the comb so that you can repeat this procedure until all the pepper has been separated from the salt!

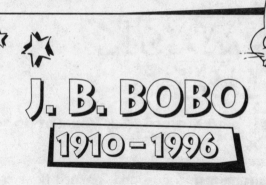

J. B. BOBO
1910 – 1996

J. B. Bobo is the author of Modern
Coin Magic, every coin magician's
reference book and bible. His family
name was originally Beaubeaux, but
was changed to Bobo when they
emigrated to America. He was born
in Texas, but spent his youth in
Canada. After a career as a window
display decorator he became a full
time magician and in 1952
completed his classic book for which
he is known to magicians
around the world.

A MAGIC CODE

This is a great word trick you can do with any mirror.

Requirements:

A MIRROR, A SHEET OF PAPER AND A PEN OR PENCIL.

On the sheet of paper write the words "A MAGIC CODE". It is important that you write this in capitals; otherwise it will not work!

Hold the sheet of paper, the correct way up, in front of the mirror. In the mirror, you will see that all the words are reversed. However, if you turn the piece of paper upside-down, amazingly the letters of the word "CODE" can be read in the reflection, even though all the others will be jumbled.

This will work with any words which contain only the letters B, C, D, E, H, I, K, O and X. What other suitable words can you come up with? What is the longest possible word?

BLOWING OVER A BRICK

It seems impossible, but you really can blow over a heavy brick!

Requirements:

A HOUSE BRICK AND A ROUND BALLOON.

Stand the house brick up on one short end on any strong surface (This is one stunt that it might be better to do outside, rather than on your dining table!). Challenge any of your friends to blow over the brick. Of course, however much they huff and puff, they won't be able to blow it over.

The balloon is the secret to this intriguing puzzle. When everybody has run out of breath and wants to know how it can be done, place the balloon under the short end of the brick (see illustration). All you have to do now is blow up the balloon and this will tip over the brick. It's simple, when you know the secret!

UNBURSTABLE BALLOONS

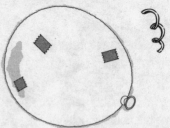

Even though everybody knows it is impossible, you are able to sticks pins and needles into an inflated balloon, as though it were a pincushion!

Requirements:

A ROUND BALLOON, PINS AND/OR NEEDLES AND CLEAR TAPE.

Secret preparation: Before your performance, blow up the balloon and stick small patches of clear tape on to the balloon (see illustration).

When you perform the trick simply make sure that you push the needles and pins through the tape patches into the balloon. Amazingly these prevent the balloon from bursting.

However, the patches do not prevent the balloon from deflating when you have removed the pins and needles!

So, as soon as you have removed them, stick one into an untaped part of the balloon to burst it and prove that it is a real balloon!

You could use "patter" about hypnotizing the balloon so that it feels no pain and then wake it from its "hypnotic sleep" before you burst it. You could even draw eyes, a nose and a mouth on the balloon to make a face and give it a personality. What other presentations can you think of?

SEEING THROUGH A BRICK

This is more of a scientific experiment than a magic trick, but it is amazing – and great fun!

Requirements:
A HOUSE BRICK, MODELLING CLAY AND FOUR SMALL HAND MIRRORS.

Even though it doesn't sound possible you can actually see through the centre of a solid house brick. You will need to set up the four mirrors exactly as illustrated, using the modelling clay to hold them in exactly the correct position.

When you have done this it is possible to look in the first mirror and see a reflection of what is on the other side of the brick. It appears as though you can see through the centre of it!

With the set-up in place, you can – by pointing a flashlight at the first mirror – apparently shine a beam of light through solid brick!

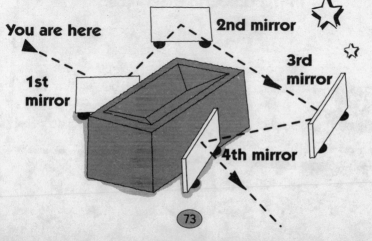

You are here

2nd mirror

3rd mirror

1st mirror

4th mirror

ROSS BERTRAM
1912–1992

Bertram was considered by
magicians to be the true heir to
T. Nelson Downs' throne – the
new 'King of Koins'. He was
born in Toronto, Canada. He
made his big impact upon the
magic world when he first
appeared at magic conventions
in the U.S.A. in the 1940s.

THE MIND- READING BANANA

Your friends select a number. A normal-looking banana is peeled to reveal that, although the skin is completely unharmed, the banana is split into the selected number of pieces! The banana has obviously read their minds!

Requirements:

ONE BANANA, A LONG NEEDLE, A PACK OF PLAYING CARDS AND AN OPAQUE HANDKERCHIEF.

Secret preparation: In fact, you decide how many pieces you want and secretly cut them beforehand. To cut a banana while it is still inside its skin takes some practice, but it is worth it for the amazing bizarre result. Imagine the look on someone's face when they peel a banana and find it cut into several sections!

You use the needle to cut the sections. Insert it in one of the dark lines that divide two sections of the banana skin and push it into the banana inside. Ensure that the needle does not come out of the skin on the other side. Sharply wiggle the needle back and forth. Like wire cutting through cheese, the needle will cut

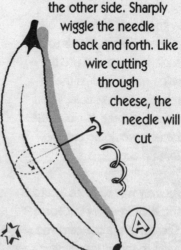

75

through the soft banana pulp.

You can repeat this at various points up and down the banana, depending on how many cut sections you want inside. This is the secret preparation necessary to cut the banana.

To make your friends choose the number you require, you will need to "force" it on them. In a force, the audience believes that they have a free choice, but in fact, the magician makes them take that decision!

A good way to force a low number for this trick is to force a playing card and use the value of the card as the number. For example, if you force the three of clubs, the banana would be cut into three pieces.

An easy way to force a card is the **Handkerchief Cut Force**. Secretly place the card you want to force (let's assume that

it is the three of clubs) on top of the face-down pack. In performance, fan through the cards to show that they are all different, then square up the pack and hold them face down in one hand. With the other hand cover the pack with an opaque handkerchief (Fig.A). Under the cover of this, secretly turn over the pack as you ask one of your friends to cut the cards through the material of the handkerchief (Fig. B).

When they have cut the cards, turn the cards remaining in your hand back face down and ask your friend to lift away the handkerchief and the cards they "cut" so that everybody can see which card they cut to. Turn over the top card of the portion in your hand – it will be the force card. Take the handkerchief – with the portion of the pack that was "cut" still inside – so that no one can see that the cards inside are actually face up! (Fig. C).

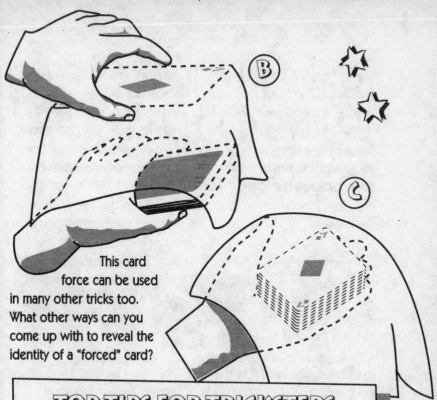

This card force can be used in many other tricks too. What other ways can you come up with to reveal the identity of a "forced" card?

TOP TIPS FOR TRICKSTERS

Palming - When secretly concealing an object in your hand (known as palming) the most important thing is to make your hand look natural. If your hand looks tense and cramped it will be noticed. The best advice is to keep something "palmed" in your hand all day (like a coin) so that you forget about it. When you forget about it you cannot unconsciously draw attention to it!

CHANGING DIRECTION

A glass of water causes an arrow to point in the opposite direction!

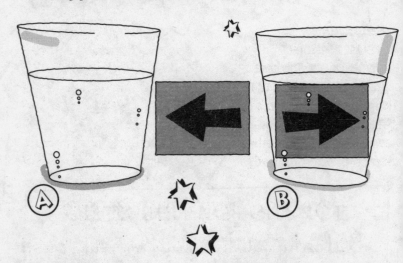

A

B

Requirements:

A CLEAR GLASS TUMBLER FILLED WITH WATER AND A SMALL FOLDED PIECE OF CARD (SMALLER THAN THE WIDTH OF THE GLASS) WITH A BOLD ARROW DRAWN ON IT, POINTING TO YOUR LEFT (FIG. A).

You can make the arrow point in the completely opposite direction simply by placing the small piece of card behind the glass and looking at the arrow through the water. Amazingly, the arrow that you know is pointing to the left (after all, it was you that drew it!) is now pointing to the right (Fig. B).

Ask your science teacher how this works, because I don't know – I just know that it does!

WATER TO WINE

You cause a glass full of clear water to change into a bright red liquid!

Requirements:

A GLASS TUMBLER FULL OF WATER, A FOLDING CARDBOARD SCREEN LARGE ENOUGH TO COVER THE GLASS, SOME THIN WIRE, A SMALL PIECE OF SPONGE AND SOME WATER-BASED RED PAINT.

Secret preparation: Using the wire, attach the sponge to the inside of the screen so that, when it is placed in front of the glass, the sponge will be dunked into the water (Fig. A). Just before your performance, cover the sponge with the paint.

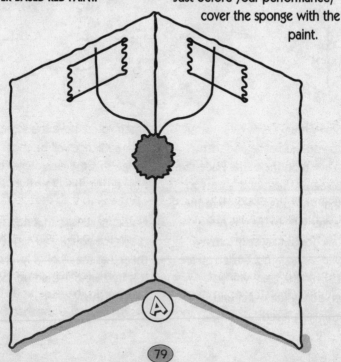

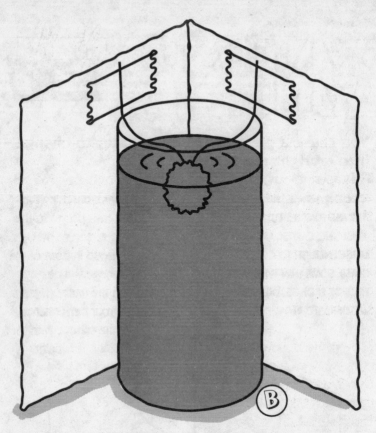

(B)

Show the glass of clear water to your audience and then place it on the table. Place the screen in front of the glass so that the sponge goes into the water (Fig. B). At this point, talk about magically turning water into wine. While you are talking, the paint will be colouring the water and changing it red!

When you remove the screen, your audience will be shocked to see that the clear water has now turned bright red!

Please make sure that nobody drinks the liquid! You can tell them that the alcohol level of this "red wine" would be too high for them!

THREE COINS IN A WINE GLASS?

This is a great challenge that you can use to amaze your friends – and win some money at the same time.

Requirements:

A WINE GLASS (FILLED RIGHT TO THE BRIM WITH WATER) AND A STACK OF PENNIES.

Ask your friends how many coins they think they could drop into the wine glass before the water overflows. Because the glass is filled right to the brim they will probably say just two or three. In fact, if you drop the coins into the glass in a special way, you can get up to 70 coins in!

You must slide the coins into the glass down its inner side. If you do it this way, you will actually see the water rise up above the rim of the glass and still not overflow. This incredibly bizarre sight is the result of the water's surface tension.

If your friends guess a low number (like two or three), you may be able to get them to agree to pay you a sum for every coin above their guess that you add without the water overflowing. If they agree, you'll soon be rich!

FLOATING NEEDLE

You can make a needle float on the surface of a glass of water.

Requirements:

A GLASS OF WATER, A NEEDLE AND A SMALL SQUARE OF TISSUE PAPER.

To achieve the bizarre sight of a needle floating on the surface of the water requires a little set-up. Float the tissue paper on the surface of the water and gently place the needle on top of the paper.

Now **very gently push** down on the tissue paper. The paper will sink into the glass, but the needle will magically remain floating on the surface. Incredible!

CLASSROOM TRICKS

This chapter is full of fun tricks you can perform to fool and amaze your teachers and friends at school.

URI GELLER PEN

You can show off your incredible psychic powers by causing a pen to bend visibly, as though it were made of rubber.

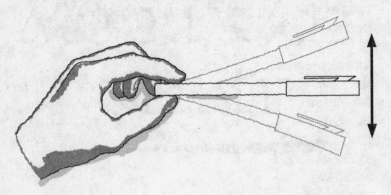

Requirements:
ALL THAT YOU NEED IS A REGULAR PEN. THE TRICK IS EVEN MORE IMPRESSIVE IF YOU BORROW THIS FROM A FRIEND.

This is actually an optical illusion. The pen doesn't bend at all, but if you do it correctly it looks amazingly realistic.

It is very important that you handle the pen correctly to make it work. Hold it very loosely between your thumb and index finger, as in the illustration. Quickly move your hand up and down a little way. It might take a while to develop the correct speed and movement, but when you do, it will look as though the pen is made of rubber.

THE STRETCHING BOOMERANGS

This is a great one to fool your science teacher or anyone who believes it is impossible to stretch and shrink cardboard!

Requirements:

YOU WILL NEED TO MAKE OUT OF CARDBOARD TWO IDENTICALLY SIZED BOOMERANGS TO MATCH THOSE ILLUSTRATED (FIG. A). THE EASIEST WAY TO DO THIS IS TO TRACE THE ILLUSTRATIONS AND, USING A PIECE OF CARBON PAPER, TRACE THE SHAPES ON TO THIN CARDBOARD. YOU CAN THEN CUT THESE OUT AND START AMAZING FOLK.

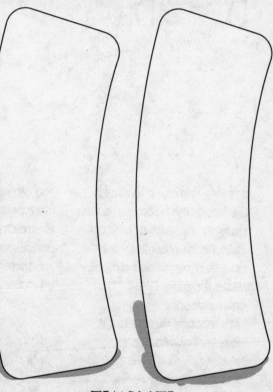

TEMPLATE

Ⓐ

It is easy to make it look as if the size of the boomerangs has changed. If you hold them up against each other, they are the same size, but if you hold one above the other (Fig. B), the lower one appears bigger. It's just an optical illusion, but it looks very convincing.

You can make this illusion even more persuasive by pretending to stretch or squeeze the boomerangs physically before you show them larger or smaller.

THE FLOATING PEN

A pen seems to float between your hands, defying gravity!

Requirements:

A REGULAR PEN.

Place the pen to be floated flat on the desk in front of you.

To perform this, you need to interweave your fingers so that your right third finger is concealed behind your left palm (Fig. A). To achieve this, point the fingers of both hands

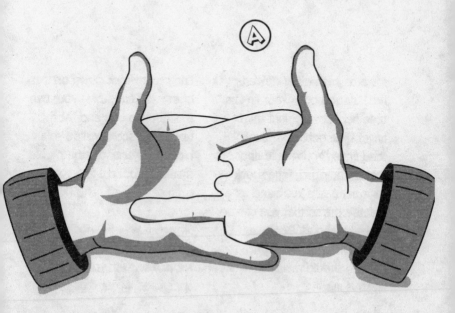

(A)

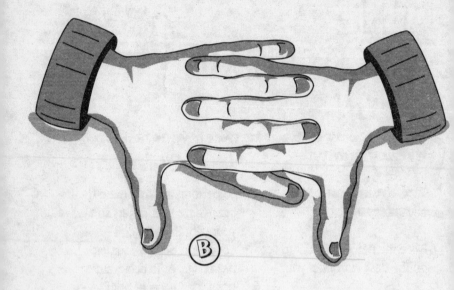

(B)

towards each other (fingertips first). As you bring your fingers together, let your right third finger slide behind your left third finger. You should find that all the other fingers lock together easily. You need to practise this so that you can do it quickly and easily. Seeing your hands from the front, nobody should realize that one finger is missing!

Bring your hands down on top of the pen and, using your two thumbs, grip one end. At the same time, secretly slide your hidden finger under the pen so that it is clipped against the palm of your left hand (Fig. B).

Slowly lift your interlocked hands from the table until they are parallel with your chest. It appears as if your thumbs are

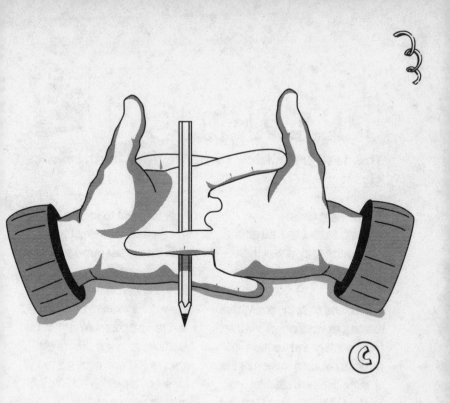

holding the pen. When your hands are in front of you, move both your thumbs away from the pen leaving it apparently floating behind your hands. If you watch this in a mirror, you will see how magical it looks.

To finish the trick, bend your right third finger inwards so that the pen is released and drops to your desk. Everybody will want to check the pen to make sure there is nothing sticky on it! As they do this, separate your hands; then you can allow your friends to examine them, too!

1089 PREDICTION

This is a great trick to baffle your mathematics class!

Requirements:

YOU WILL NEED A PEN, PAPER, A CALCULATOR AND A PREDICTION WITH 1089 WRITTEN ON IT.

Ask a friend to help you. Ask this assistant to write down any three-figure number and, to make it harder for you, to make sure that all three digits are different – for example, 749. It is important that you do not see this number or any of the following calculations.

Tell your assistant to write the reverse of the selected number below it, so that the first digit goes last, the middle digit stays where it is and the last digit goes first. In our example, that would be 947. Now tell them to subtract the smaller number from the larger number and write down the answer. In our example, 947 – 749 = 198.

Now tell them to reverse the three-figure answer just as they did with the first number and add that to the previous answer. (If they only have a two-figure answer, tell them to double it and reverse that number.) In our example, reversing the answer gives us 891 and adding it to 198 gives us – amazingly – 1089, the number written on the prediction!

As long as you give your assistant these instructions, in this order, the final total will always equal 1089. It's amazing, but it always works.

To add an extra surprise to this, you could write your prediction as 6801. At the end, it appears that you have got it wrong – until you turn the prediction upside down!

① 749
9 4 7

② 947
749−
198

③ 198
891+
= 1089

THE STICKY RULER

To the amazement of your friends and teachers you cause an ordinary ruler to adhere to the palm of your hand!

Requirements:
TWO RULERS AND A WRISTWATCH.

Fig. A shows the hidden view of this old trick. You grip your left wrist with your right hand and hold the ruler against your left palm by secretly extending

the second finger of your right hand. From the front, nobody will notice that there are only three fingers of your right hand wrapped around your wrist.

The following version is even better, requiring only one

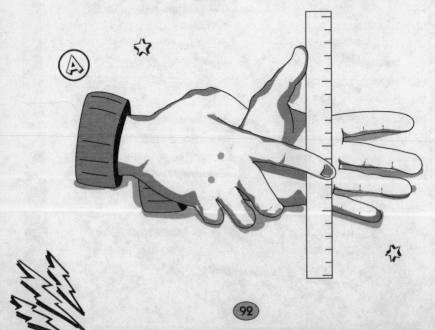

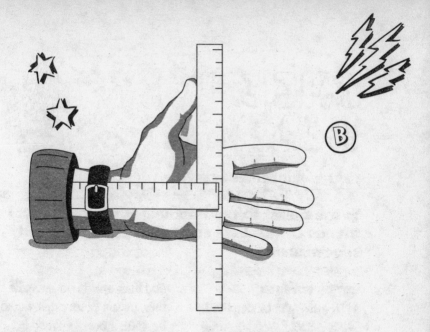

hand, and will fool anybody who knows the old way!

Secretly slide one of the rulers up your left sleeve so that it goes under your watch strap. You want the end of the ruler to reach about the middle of the palm of your left hand. This ruler will do the job that your right finger does in the old version. When the secret ruler is in position and completely hidden from your audience, you can begin your performance. Remember to keep your left hand palm down; otherwise the trick is not very impressive!

Close your left hand into a loose fist. With your right hand, slide one end of the other ruler into the hole formed by the thumb of your left fist, and push it through the closed fist. Make sure that, as you push it through, it gets trapped between the hidden ruler and the palm of your hand. When equal amounts of the ruler are sticking out both sides of your fist (easy to measure with a ruler!), remove your right hand and slowly open your fist (Fig. B). Amazingly the ruler sticks to your hand as if by magic!

MIND-READING MATHEMATICS

You are able to read the minds of your school friends or teachers and reveal their ages and shoe sizes!

Requirements:

A PEN AND PAPER OR CALCULATOR.

Ask a friend to write down their shoe size or punch it into the calculator (For example, 2). It is important that, throughout, you do not see any of the figures or calculations. Otherwise it would not be mind-reading – it would be cheating!

Then ask them to double this number (that is, multiply it by 2) and add 5 to the total (in our example, this makes 9). Next tell them to multiply this by 50 and

add their age (in our example if they are ten years old, it would be 460).

Finally, they must add the number of days in a year: 365. Ask them to tell you the total (in our example, 825). From this information, you can tell them their age and shoe size!

All that you have to do is secretly subtract 615 from the total. The first figure or figures of the total will be their shoe size and the last figure or figures will be their age. In our example 825 – 615 =210. 2 is the shoe size, 10 is the age!

BUATIER DE KOLTA
(1847-1903)

This French-born magician was
probably the most creative and
inventive magician of the 1800s. He
invented the Vanishing Birdcage (as
made famous by Carl Hertz), the Vanish
of a Lady as she sat in a chair, the
production of flowers from an empty
paper cone and The Expanding Die, in
which a small die (die is the singular of
dice) visibly grew until a woman
climbed out of it!

THE VANISHING PENCIL

Whenever you are bored with schoolwork, you can make your pencil vanish!

Requirements:
A SHORT PENCIL.

For this trick, you need to have your "spectator" on your left. Ask them to hold out their right hand, palm up. With your left hand, hold on to their right wrist. Hold the pencil in your right hand (Fig. A).

Lift the pencil up and bring it down to tap the spectator's open hand. Explain that, on the count of three, something amazing is going to happen in their hand!

Swing your right hand up in an

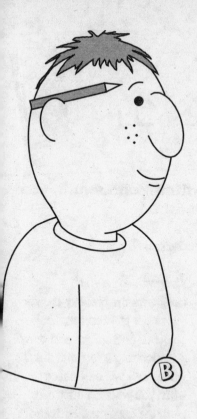

"two" as you tap their palm again.

The next time your hand swings up, you leave the pencil tucked behind your ear (Fig. B). The timing must be the same as before – the right hand swings back down as though nothing has happened.

As you bring your hand down, point your index finger and tap it on the spectator's hand as you say "three". The pencil has vanished!

When you want to make the pencil reappear, you can show your empty right hand, reach behind your ear and, bringing the pencil forward, reveal it – apparently having produced it from mid-air!

arc to the right of your face and back down. Count "one" as the end of the pencil taps the spectator's open hand. Repeat this action and count

QUICK-CHANGING CHALK

A white piece of chalk writes a different colour!

Requirements:

A PIECE OF CHALK (NOT WHITE) AND SOME WHITE CORRECTING FLUID.

Secret preparation: You need to "paint" the piece of chalk with the correcting fluid, but leave one end uncovered. When the fluid dries, it will look like a piece of white chalk.

When you show your classmates the piece of chalk, remember to keep the coloured end hidden and draw attention to the fact that it is white. They will be amazed when you write on the board (with the unpainted end) and produce a different colour!

TOP TIPS FOR TRICKSTERS

Never reveal the secret behind your tricks. If you can do the tricks people will think you are special and have magical powers - if they know that anybody can do it they will be less impressed.

STRONG PAPER

This is one for your woodwork class. A single sheet of writing paper enables you to snap a wooden ruler in half!

Requirements:

A WOODEN RULER, A HAMMER AND A SINGLE SHEET OF WRITING PAPER.

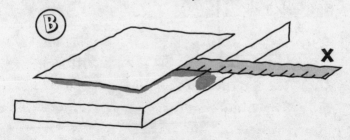

Balance the ruler over the edge of a workbench (Fig. A). Place the sheet of paper on top of the portion of the ruler that is on the bench. Now, using the hammer, hit the ruler at the point marked X (Fig. B).

You would expect the ruler to flip up into the air, taking the paper with it, but in fact, the single sheet of paper is strong enough to hold the ruler in position and cause the ruler to snap in half!

CHECKERED PAINT!

You can have great fun in your art class, as you demonstrate your magical checkered paint, which impossibly paints perfect black and white checks!

Requirements:

WHITE PAPER, BLACK WATER-BASED PAINT AND WHITE WAX CRAYON.

Secret preparation: To create this impossible artwork, you need to prepare the paper in advance by using the white wax crayon to draw and fill in symmetrical white squares (Fig. A).

Because you have used white crayon on white paper, it will look just like a piece of regular paper. However, when you paint on it with the black paint, the white squares will appear through the black paint. This will create the impression that you are using magical checkered paint!

Ⓐ

VANISHING PAINT

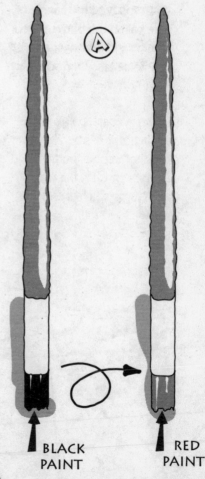

This is another fun stunt to fool your art class
– you appear to make wet paint vanish from
your fist.

Requirements:

AN OLD, THICK, ROUND-ENDED
PAINTBRUSH AND BLACK AND RED
PAINT.

Secret preparation: This trick
relies on two secret factors –
special sleight of hand and a
gimmicked paint brush. Don't
worry about the sleight of hand.
It's easy to do and I'll teach it to
you in a second, but first you
need to make the gimmicked
brush.

Dip the bristles of the paintbrush
into black paint, then allow it to
dry. When it is completely hard,
you can continue. On one side
of the brush paint some red
paint, so that it looks as though
the brush has been dipped in
red paint (Fig. A). It is

BLACK
PAINT

RED
PAINT

important that no red paint gets onto the other side of the brush. Wait for this to dry, too. When it has, you are ready to move on to the secret move.

This is called the "paddle move" and is shown in Figs B–D. You twist the handle of the paintbrush between your thumb and forefinger and, at the same time, turn your hand to apparently show the other side of the brush. The result is that there appears to be the same shade of paint on both sides. Practise until you have learned to do this move well as it is essential to the success of this trick.

To perform the trick, use the paddle move to show that there is red paint on both sides of the brush. Close your other hand into a fist around the bristles and pretend to squeeze the paint out of the brush and into your hand. As you do this, secretly twist the handle of the brush with the other hand. When you pull the brush out of your fist, only

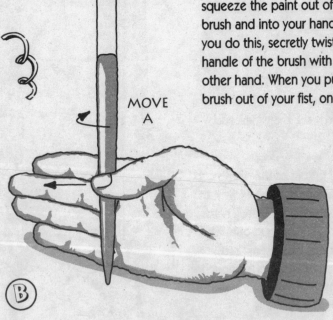

MOVE
A

B

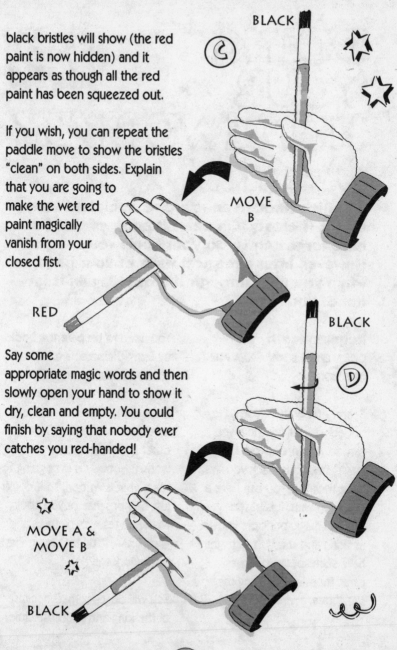

black bristles will show (the red paint is now hidden) and it appears as though all the red paint has been squeezed out.

If you wish, you can repeat the paddle move to show the bristles "clean" on both sides. Explain that you are going to make the wet red paint magically vanish from your closed fist.

BLACK

MOVE B

RED

Say some appropriate magic words and then slowly open your hand to show it dry, clean and empty. You could finish by saying that nobody ever catches you red-handed!

BLACK

MOVE A & MOVE B

BLACK

DOING YOUR HOMEWORK BY MAGIC

You flick through an exercise book and show that it is empty. Oh dear! It appears that you have forgotten to do your homework. However, after a magical wave of your hand, when you flick through the book again it is full of your work!

Requirements:

ONE EXERCISE BOOK AND A PAIR OF SCISSORS.

Secret preparation: Sorry, I'm not able to tell you how you can do your homework by magic, but I can teach you this great trick that you can have a lot of fun with. It is based on a classical magic principle known as "long and short". You might have seen special packs of cards for sale employing the same idea.

You need to prepare the book by using the scissors to cut about 1/2 inch (1 cm) off the edge of every other page (see illustration). Now comes the hard part: you have to fill every other two page spread with writing! Nobody is ever going to read what is written, so it could just be nonsense or you could fill the pages with pictures and graphs. Anything that looks like homework will do!

You will discover that, because of the long-and-short principle,

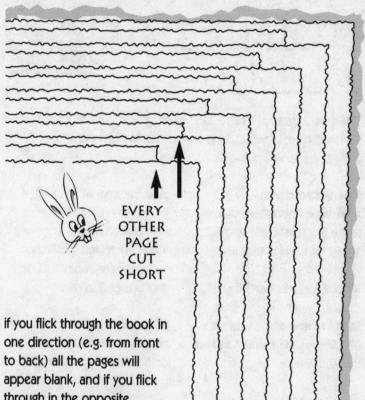

EVERY
OTHER
PAGE
CUT
SHORT

if you flick through the book in one direction (e.g. from front to back) all the pages will appear blank, and if you flick through in the opposite direction (e.g. from back to front) it will appear to be full! Take this specially prepared book with you to school and you will be all set to amaze your teachers and classmates. When your teacher asks for your homework, flick through the book to show that it is empty. Then explain that this is not a problem because you are

a magician! Make a magical pass over the book, and when you flick through again (in the other direction of course!), it will be full!

This is a great trick. Look out for other variations on the same principle later in this book.

BALANCING RULER

This is another one for the woodwork class. You cause a wooden ruler to balance on the edge of a workbench.

Requirements:

A HAMMER, A WOODEN RULER (DO NOT USE A PLASTIC RULER – IT WILL SNAP!) AND AN ELASTIC BAND.

Wrap the elastic band tightly around the end of the ruler. Slide the end of the hammer's handle into the elastic band so that the hammer hangs down from the ruler at an angle. If the other end of the ruler is now placed on the edge of a workbench, you should find that the ruler appears to defy gravity (see illustration).

With a bit of practice, you could even balance the ruler on the end of one finger!

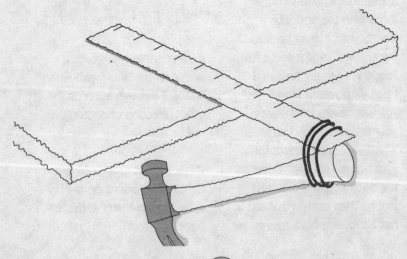

PROFESSOR HOFFMANN
(1839 - 1919)

Professor Hoffmann was the pen-name of Angelo Lewis, a professional barrister and journalist, and was for many years Britain's leading magical author. The first coin tricks to be described in detail appeared in his books. His books are now rarities, sought by magical collectors everywhere. They included Modern Magic, More Magic, Later Magic and Magical Titbits.

RISING PENCIL IN TEST TUBE

You cause a pencil to rise mysteriously inside a sealed test tube!

TO
BUTTON

(A)

Requirements:

A SMALL PENCIL, NON-PERMANENT ADHESIVE, BLACK THREAD, SCISSORS, A TEST TUBE AND A RUBBER STOPPER.

Secret preparation: One end of the thread is secretly attached to the end of the pencil with the adhesive. The other end of the thread is wrapped around a button on your shirt or blouse (Fig. A). Also, use the scissors to make a small nick in the rubber stopper so that the thread can run through (Fig. B).

Place the pencil inside the test tube and put the stopper in place. Slowly move your body away from the test tube. You will see the pencil rising inside, being pulled by the thread that runs from your button through the nick in the stopper to the bottom of the pencil. You may have to experiment with the length of the thread so that all this happens smoothly and discreetly.

Once all your apparatus is set up, it is probably best to store everything in a shirt pocket so that you don't have to connect up the thread when you perform.

After you have amazed your friends by causing the pencil to move around mysteriously inside the test tube, you can hand out everything for examination. First, hand out the test tube and stopper, and while they are being checked, secretly peel the adhesive off the end of the pencil so that can be examined, too!

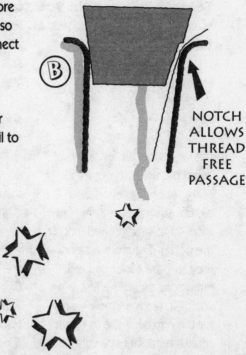

NOTCH
ALLOWS
THREAD
FREE
PASSAGE

KIM'S SECRET

I'm sure you've played "Kim's Game", even if you didn't know that that is what it is called! It's the game where you are shown a number of small objects for a few seconds before they are covered and one removed. You are then challenged to remember what is missing. "Kim's Secret" will enable you to win this game every time – and remember all kinds of other things, too!

Requirements:

NONE, NOT EVEN A GOOD MEMORY.

This works by the formation of 'word pictures' in your mind. Using your imagination, you picture strange scenes in your mind – the stranger and funnier the better. The more bizarre they are, the easier you will remember them. The first thing you must learn are new words for the numbers one to ten. It sounds hard, but I promise it's not – as all the words rhyme, it shouldn't take you long!

1 = Bun

2 = Shoe

3 = Key

4 = Door

5 = Hive (of bees)

6 = Sticks

7 = Heaven (imagine clouds)

8 = Gate

9 = Sunshine

10 = Pen

When you are shown the ten objects, you just have to feature each one in a weird word picture, after assigning it a different number. For example, if there is a small teddy bear, imagine him eating a bun or being chased by bees. When the objects are revealed the second time, just go through the numbers in order until you find something missing.

You can use the same system to impress your classmates. Ask someone to write the numbers 1 to 10 in a column on the board. Now ask people to call out objects to be written next to each number. As they do this, you form suitable word pictures in your mind.

Now, when all ten objects have been chosen (one for each number), you can stand with your back to the board and call them off in order. You will also find that, with practice, you can remember the list backwards and can even let someone call out a number between 1 and 10 and instantly be able to tell them the object alongside it.

This is a really impressive stunt and well worth the small amount of effort required.

I KNOW YOUR NUMBERS

This is another great mind-reading trick.

Requirements:

A PAD OF BLANK PAPER, A
PIECE OF PAPER AND AN
ENVELOPE, A PEN AND
A CALCULATOR.

THREE DIFFERENT TYPES
OF HANDWRITING!

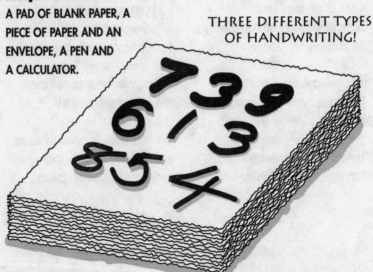

Secret preparation: This trick
requires some setting up.
Before your performance you
need to "gimmick" the pad of
paper. First, you need to make
the pad "double-sided". Both
sides must be exactly the same.

This might mean that you need
to make special identical
covers for both sides.

On the back of the pad, write
three different three-figure
numbers in a column (see

illustration). When you perform the trick, you are going to pretend that these numbers were written by different people, so you might want to write each of them in slightly different handwriting. Add up these three numbers, but don't write the total on the pad. This number is going to be your prediction. Write it on another piece of paper that you seal inside the envelope. Now turn the pad over so that the blank side is showing.

To begin your performance, hand your prediction envelope to a member of your audience and tell them to hold it safely.

Now hand the pad (blank side up remember!) and pen to another audience member and ask them to write down any three-figure number. Take back the pad and pen and hand them to a different member of your audience and ask them to write another three-figure

number underneath the first. Again pass the pad and pen to somebody else for the last three-figure number to be written. When they have done this, take the pen and pad and explain that you need someone who is good at addition to total up the numbers. This is when you might need your calculator!

It is important that the person who does the adding up is not sitting near the three who wrote down the numbers, as you are about to switch those numbers for the ones that you secretly wrote before the show! To do this, turn the pad over as you walk towards the person who is going to add them up. Of course, this means that their total will be the same as your prediction!

After this person has added up the numbers, ask them to call out the total and have the envelope containing your prediction opened to prove it is correct!

OVER THE TEACHER'S HEAD

This trick – invented by the famous American magician Harry Blackstone Sr – is perfect if you have to do a big show at school, because everybody can see how the trick is done . . . except the teacher helping you!

Requirements:

A CHAIR AND A BOX OF TISSUES.

Sit the teacher on the chair facing the audience and place the box of tissues on the teacher's knees. It is important that you stand to your teacher's left. Remove one of the tissues and roll it up into a ball. You are going to make the ball vanish by throwing it over your teacher's left shoulder. The way that you do this is very similar to The Vanishing Pencil trick, described earlier in this chapter.

Hold the tissue ball in your right hand and hold your left hand flat in front of your teacher (see illustration). Explain that you will put the tissue ball in your left hand on the count of three. Tap the ball against your left hand and say "one". Lift your right hand up in an arc over your teacher's left shoulder so it goes just out of their sight.

Tap the ball on your left hand again as you say "two". This time, when you lift up your right hand out of your teacher's sight, you actually throw the ball on the floor behind them! Don't be surprised if this makes the rest of your audience laugh, because they have seen how the teacher is about to be fooled!

You must continue at the same speed as you move your empty right hand back to tap on your left hand. Close your left hand into a fist, as if it really does contain the tissue and ask your teacher to blow on your fist. They will be amazed when you open your left hand and it is empty!

This is very funny, as everybody else knows where the tissue ball went. It is one of the few tricks that can be repeated, since every time you do it, it becomes funnier and funnier. However, if you do want to repeat it, you must practise a lot, because every time your teacher is going to be watching closer and closer!

Some magicians finish this trick by making the box of tissues vanish over the head of their assisting audience member!

BOBBY BERNARD

Bobby Bernard is one of British magic's best known teachers, having produced many award winning acts. He is also well known in magical circles for his skill and innovative creations in the field of sleight of hand with coins. His stage act is a theatrical presentation of the magic of Isaac Fawkes the well known magician from the 1800's.

MAGIC IN THE PLAY-GROUND

This chapter is full of tricks you can do outside with pocket money, skipping ropes, handkerchiefs – and your body! There are also a few you can do inside to brighten up a wet playtime!

ONE-HANDED KNOT

Your friends will be baffled by your ability to tie a knot in a length of rope with one hand!

Requirements:

A LENGTH OF ROPE ABOUT 30 INCHES (75 CM) LONG.

Secret preparation: Tie a knot at one end of the rope.

Dangle the rope from your right hand, keeping the knot concealed inside your hand (Fig. A). We will refer to the knotted end of the rope as end A and the unknotted end as end B.

Explain to your audience that after hours of practice you have finally mastered the toughest sleight of hand trick –

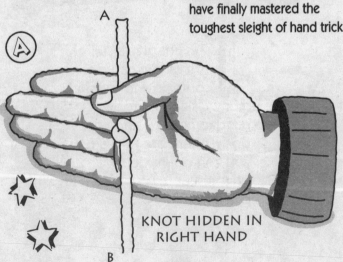

Ⓐ

A

B

KNOT HIDDEN IN RIGHT HAND

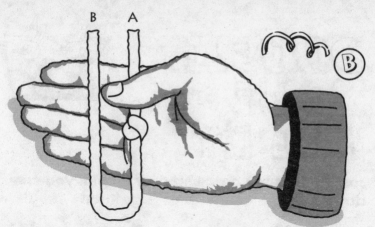

you can tie a knot in a rope using just one hand! Clip end B between the index and second fingers of your right hand (Fig. B). Shake the rope and, at the same time, release end B. You have failed! Explain that this proves how difficult it is.

Offer to attempt to do it again. Once again, bring end B up to your right hand and clip it between your fingers. Shake the rope but, this time, hold on to end B and release end A (Fig. C). It seems that you have magically tied a knot in the end of the rope with just one hand. All those hours of practice paid off!

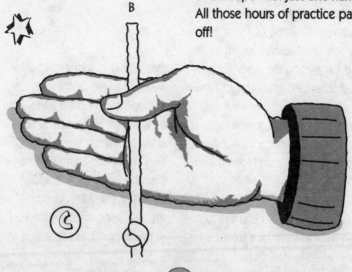

DOUBLE YOUR MONEY

Just by waving your hand over a coin, you can double it!

Requirements:
TWO COINS OF THE
SAME VALUE.

Secret preparation: One of the coins is held by the edges horizontally between the right thumb and second finger. Hold the other coin between the tips of the right thumb and second finger, at right angles to the first coin, so that it faces the audience. Figs A and B show the position of both coins. If you look at this set-up in a mirror, you will see how the front coin hides the coin behind it.

It is important that you practise this trick in front of a mirror so that you know where your friends can be positioned without seeing both coins. The trick is best if the coin is held at the audience's eye level. It is also important to make sure that the edge of the hidden coin is at the exact centre of the visible coin. This gives you as much cover as possible.

To perform the trick, hold up your right hand, apparently showing one coin between your thumb and second finger.

Show both sides of your left hand to prove you have no extra coins hidden.

Bring the two hands together, with the tips of the fingers and thumbs of both hands pointing towards each other. Remember to keep your hands at the audience's eye level so they do not see the extra coin.

Your left thumb pushes on the edge of the visible coin pivoting it on the hidden coin so that both coins lie flat against each other. Take one coin in each hand. Separate your hands to show your amazed friends that you have doubled your money!

B

TOP TIPS FOR TRICKSTERS

If you want to put together an act to perform on stage it is a good idea to get a local drama teacher or amateur director to help you 'produce' it.

THE FRENCH DROP

This is a classic way to use sleight of hand to make a coin vanish.

Requirements:

ANY COIN.

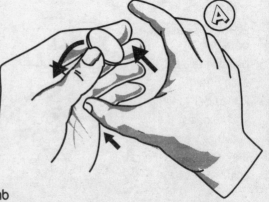

Hold the coin horizontally, parallel with the floor, between the tips of your left thumb and fingers (Fig. A). The fingers and thumb should be pointing upwards. Your fingers should be held together tightly so that there are no gaps between them; otherwise your audience might see where the coin goes!

Your right thumb goes under the coin and your right fingers cover the coin from above, as though they are about to take the coin. In fact, as soon as your right fingers conceal the coin, your right thumb releases the coin, allowing it to fall into your left hand.

However, your right hand continues to move as though it does contain the coin. It clenches into a fist and moves upwards and away to the right

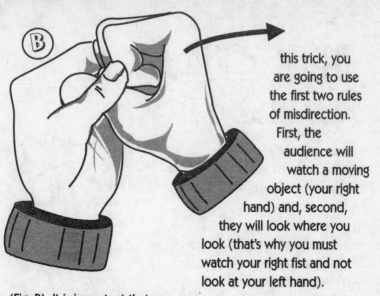

this trick, you are going to use the first two rules of misdirection. First, the audience will watch a moving object (your right hand) and, second, they will look where you look (that's why you must watch your right fist and not look at your left hand).

(Fig. B). It is important that you hold the left hand still and that your audience is aware that you are watching your right hand move.

This is known as 'misdirection'. Magicians use misdirection to direct their audiences' attention away from secrets. In

While the audience are misdirected by your right hand, close your left hand, clipping the coin at the base of the left fingers (Fig. C). (This is known as the "finger palm" position.)

Open your right hand to show that the coin has vanished!

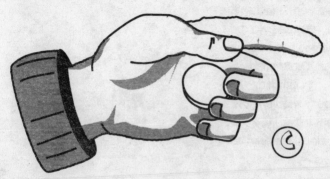

THE CHANGING MARBLE

When a marble is squeezed in your hand, it magically changes!

Requirements:

TWO MARBLES OF CONTRASTING APPEARANCE (LET'S ASSUME THAT THEY ARE RED AND BLUE).

Secret preparation: Clip the blue marble between the bases of the second and third right fingers (see illustration). Practise this until you can hold the marble in this position without your hand looking cramped. Nobody should know about this additional marble.

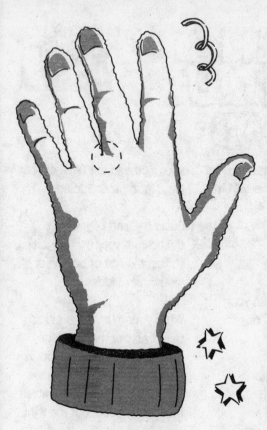

marble as described in the French Drop. This time you must be careful that the two marbles do not clink together as the two hands come together. (When props make a noise that could reveal the secret, magicians describe this as "talking".)

For this reason, it is important that the left thumb releases the red marble as soon as the right fingers cover it. The right hand closes into a fist and moves away from the left hand which has closed into a light fist to conceal the red marble inside.

This trick is based upon the French Drop move described on pages 122–3. Hold the red marble with the tips of the left hand in position for the French Drop.

Bring the right hand over the left hand, palms down, apparently to take the red

Ask someone to blow on your right fist. When you open it to show that the marble has changed from red into blue, you could joke that this is because somebody "blew" on it!

PULLING OFF YOUR THUMB

You'll have great fun shocking people with this gory trick!

Requirements:
JUST YOUR TWO HANDS!

Hold your left hand with your fingers and thumb pointing to your right and the back of your hand facing your audience (Fig. A).

Cover the end of your left thumb with your right fingertips, so that the tips of both your thumbs are hidden.

While your thumbs are hidden, secretly move their positions. Bend down the end of your left thumb so that it points to the floor. Bend your right thumb so that the tip sticks out the right side of your right fingers. It should look as though this is the tip of your left thumb.

(A)

126

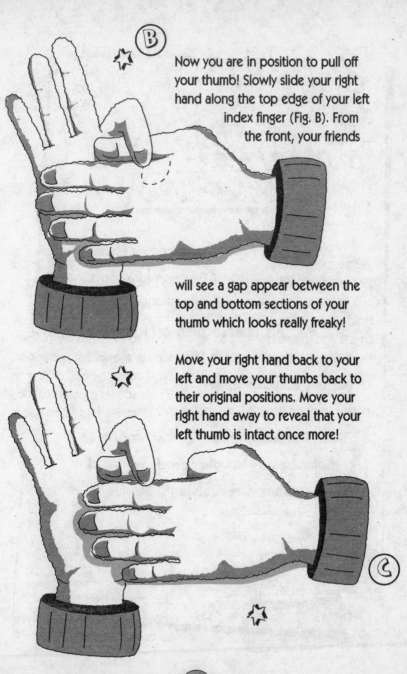

Now you are in position to pull off your thumb! Slowly slide your right hand along the top edge of your left index finger (Fig. B). From the front, your friends

will see a gap appear between the top and bottom sections of your thumb which looks really freaky!

Move your right hand back to your left and move your thumbs back to their original positions. Move your right hand away to reveal that your left thumb is intact once more!

KALANAG
1893-1963

Kalanag was the stage name of Helmut
Schreiber a rotund German illusionist.
After the Second World War he toured the
world with his spectacular, exciting illusion
show 'Sim Sala Bim' (the same name as
Dante's touring show). His show is now in
the collection of popular British magician,
Paul Daniels. Almost as well known as
Kalanag was his glamorous wife and
number one assistant, Gloria.

JUMPING BAND

A rubber band travels invisibly on your hand.

Requirements:

A RUBBER BAND.

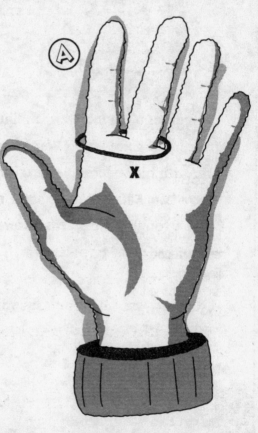

Place the rubber band over the first two fingers of your left hand (Fig. A). With your right thumb and index finger, grab the band at the point marked x and pull it to your right. Close your left fingers into a fist, ensuring that the tips of all four finger go inside the stretched band. Your right hand can now release its grip on the band. It will snap back on to the fingertips of the left hand (Fig. B).

From the front it appears that the band is only wrapped around your first two fingers. You should not let your audience see the situation at

rubber band of a contrasting colour to "lock" the left fingertips together (Fig. C). Even with this second band in position, the first one will still jump if you follow the above instructions!

the back. Now, just by opening the fingers of your left hand the band will jump invisibly from being around the first two fingers to around the last two. It sounds impossible, but try it yourself and you will see that it happens.

You can even take this a step further and use another

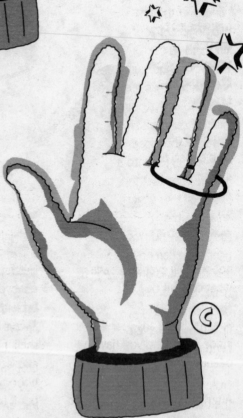

PLAYGROUND CHALLENGE

This is a great challenge for you to try on your friends. They'll never be able to answer it – unless they've got this book, too!

You hold out your closed fist and explain that it contains something that nobody in the world has ever seen before, and when they have seen it, nobody will ever see it again. What could it be?

So what is the answer? Well, inside your hand you have a peanut!

After your friends have suffered and guessed incorrectly for long enough, open your hand to show the peanut (see illustration). Break the shell to remove the nut from inside. Explain that, because it has always been covered by the shell, nobody in the world has ever seen it before. And so that nobody can ever see it again, put it in your mouth and eat it!

THE HAUNTED KEY

A mysterious-looking key turns spookily by itself!

Requirements:

A KEY, SIMILAR TO THE ONE IN FIG. A. THE OLDER AND MORE MYSTERIOUS-LOOKING IT IS THE BETTER, AS IT WILL ADD TO THE PRESENTATION.

Hold your left hand out flat and balance the key on your palm so that the end overhangs the right edge of your hand and the "teeth" of the key point towards you (Fig. B).

Now tell some suitably spooky story about finding the key in an old trunk in a cold dark attic one stormy night. Explain that you think that the key is haunted, because you are able to lock or unlock the trunk just by thinking about it.

Ask everybody to stare at the key and concentrate on getting it to unlock the trunk. As they do this, tilt your hand forwards a tiny amount . Because of the way you have balanced the key you only have to move a minute amount to make the key turn away from you. This movement of yours should not be noticed by your audience.

Spend plenty of time practising this to get the minimum amount of movement. It is worth the time spent rehearsing this for the reaction you will get from your friends when the key turns! It really is spooky – and great fun!

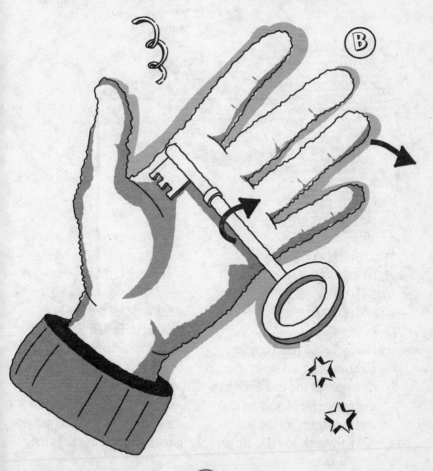

PENDULUM POWER

A pendulum dangled over your friends' hands is able to tell whether they are male or female!

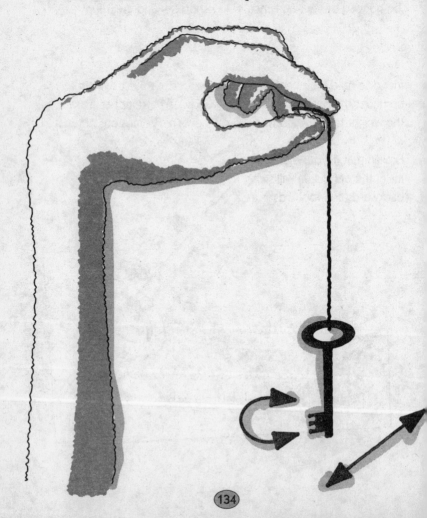

Requirements:

A 12 INCH (30 CM) LENGTH OF STRING OR CORD AND A HEAVY KEY OR SOMETHING OF A SIMILAR WEIGHT TO ACT AS A PENDULUM.

Tie the key (or whatever you are using) on to one end of the string to make a pendulum. Hold this by the unattached end of the string and ask a friend to hold their hand palm up under the pendulum. Allow the weight to swing freely.

Explain that, if your friend is male, the pendulum will swing backwards and forwards in a straight line, and if they are female, it will swing in a circle (see illustration). There is no trick to this; it will just happen!

Obviously your friends may be suspicious because you are holding the pendulum, so ask one of them to hold it and continue the experiment. As long as they allow the pendulum to just swing freely and don't attempt to make it move, nine times out of ten it will just work!

It's bizarre! Try it!

TOP TIPS FOR TRICKSTERS

Never turn your back on an audience – that's when they might sneak out!

☆

Never force your tricks on your friends. Wait until they ask to see them.

MAGIC MARBLE BAG

With this special marble bag, you can change marbles into toffees!

SIDE A

SIDE B

(A)

☆

Requirements:

THICK OPAQUE MATERIAL, A NEEDLE AND STRONG THREAD. FOR THE TRICKS, YOU WILL NEED MARBLES AND TOFFEES.

This special bag is almost like two bags sewn together. When finished, it will have two different openings. Refer to Fig. A, which shows you how to sew the material to make this. If you are (or whoever is making it for you is) particularly good at needlework, you could make the bag with a drawstring to make it look even more like a marble bag.

Once you have the bag, the tricks you can do are limited only by your imagination. For example, if you secretly put a toffee into one side of the bag, when you see your friends you could place a marble

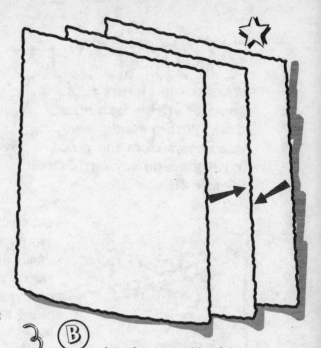

into the empty side of the bag, say some magic words and pour out the toffee from the other side. It will appear as though you have changed the marble into a toffee!

You could also use the bag to hide your secret collection of marbles or treats. What other tricks can you think of making use of your special marble bag?

OUT TO LUNCH

You show a picture of yourself sitting behind a desk. With a magic wave, you vanish from the desk, leaving a sign saying "GONE TO LUNCH".

(A)

GONE TO LUNCH

Requirements:

A STACK OF BLANK POSTCARDS, A THICK RUBBER BAND, A PEN AND SOME SCISSORS.

Secret preparation: On one of the postcards, draw or (ask someone to draw for you) a

cartoon of an empty desk with a sign saying "GONE TO LUNCH". However, it is important that this sign appears only in the top half of the picture (Fig. A). The reason for this will be revealed shortly.

You also need to cut one of the postcards in half and draw an exact duplicate of the top half of the picture, but with you apparently sitting behind the desk (Fig. B). When this half card is put on top of the first illustration it should look like a single picture. (Ignore the line going across the middle; we are going to sort that out in a second!)

Place the complete picture on top of the pile of postcards

138

and place the elastic band around the stack to hold them together. Now place the half card in position on top of the illustration and hold it in position with the rubber band (Fig. C). See, the rubber band covers that tell-tale line! Now you are all set to start.

Hold the stack of postcards with the picture pointing up. Point out to your friends that you are sitting behind your desk. Turn the stack of postcards so that the picture is pointing down and pull out the whole card picture. Make sure that you pull out the card from the correct end; otherwise you will pull out the half card – and that gives the trick away!

When you pull out the picture, the rubber band will hold the half card in position. Keep the stack facing down and get rid of them (be careful not to let anybody see the half card still under the rubber band). Keep the picture card facing downwards and make a magical pass over it. When the card is turned over, you have vanished from behind your desk and gone to lunch!

COIN THROUGH HANDKERCHIEF

You drape a handkerchief over a borrowed coin. Magically the coin visibly penetrates through the centre of the handkerchief!

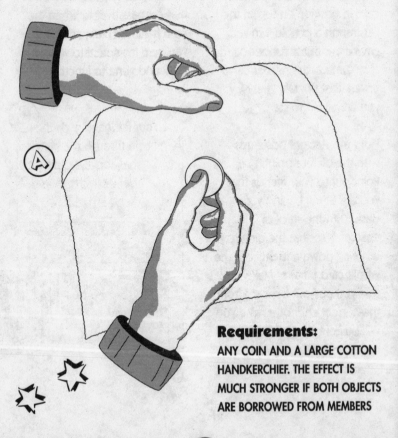

(A)

Requirements:
ANY COIN AND A LARGE COTTON HANDKERCHIEF. THE EFFECT IS MUCH STRONGER IF BOTH OBJECTS ARE BORROWED FROM MEMBERS

OF THE AUDIENCE, BUT IT IS A GOOD IDEA TO HAVE YOUR OWN COIN AND HANDKERCHIEF STANDING BY "IN THE WINGS" JUST IN CASE NOBODY HAS A CLEAN HANDKERCHIEF OR TRUSTS YOU WITH THEIR MONEY! Display the coin with the tips of your right thumb and fingers. If you have had your audience member make a mark on the coin with a pen (which will make the effect much stronger), you can now comment on their artistic ability or lack of it!

Pick up the handkerchief with your left hand and, holding it by one of the edges (not a corner), drape it over the coin and the right hand (Fig. A).

Ensure that the front edge of the handkerchief (the one nearest the spectators) drapes lower down than the back edge.

Your left hand grips the coin through the material, from above, holding it between the thumb and fingers.

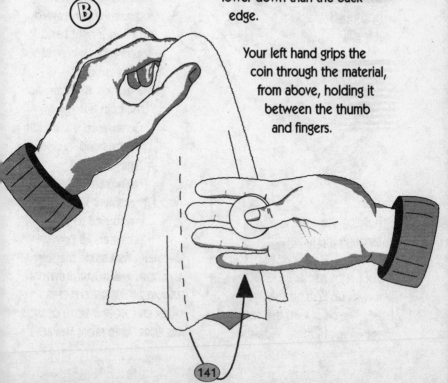

Now you remove your right hand from under the handkerchief – and secretly take the coin with it! Your right hand moves down, still holding on to the coin, below the rear edge of the handkerchief. This will not be seen by your audience because you have ensured that the front edge of the handkerchief is lower. Your left hand continues to hold the handkerchief at the centre as though it is still

holding the coin through the material!

Your right hand moves up behind the handkerchief with the coin remaining hidden. Slide the

coin under your left thumb and clip it between the thumb and the cloth.

Transfer the handkerchief and the clipped coin from the left hand to the right hand ensuring that the coin remains hidden.

The left hand slides down the handkerchief and gathers all four corners tightly together.

The left hand jerks the handkerchief downwards out of your right hand, leaving the coin held with your right fingertips. It seems that the coin has visibly penetrated the middle of the handkerchief! The coin and handkerchief are then examined and returned to their owners to prove that some magicians are trustworthy!

TOP TIPS FOR TRICKSTERS WITH SILK

It is worthwhile becoming friendly with a local seamstress. They will probably be able to make an excellent job of the various fake bags and handkerchieves described in this book and are well worth the modest charge. If you do hire somebody else to make your fake make sure that they keep the secret!

✣

Always have your own clean handkerchief to hand when doing any tricks that require one borrowed from the audience, just in case none are in a fit state for public display!

✣

When doing any effects which rely on having something hidden inside the layers of the handkerchief (i.e. coins, matches, etc.) always ensure that you do not have a direct light source behind you!

PENN JILLETTE AND TELLER

This outrageous American duo have
shocked audiences around the world
with their 'sick tricks' and upset many
magicians. They began their performing
careers as street entertainers and are
now in demand for T.V. shows and live
performances – and have even starred in
their own movie – Penn and Teller
Get Killed.

CUT AND RESTORED SKIPPING ROPE

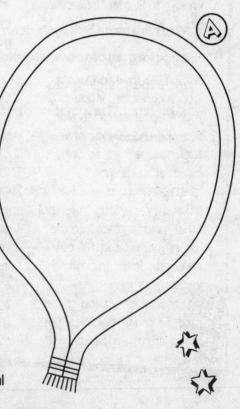

This is a great way to impress children in the playground! You cut their skipping rope into two pieces and then use your magical powers to restore it!

Requirements:
A REGULAR SKIPPING ROPE, A PAIR OF SCISSORS, A LENGTH OF ROPE 3 INCHES (7 CM) AND SOME THREAD THAT MATCHES THE COLOUR OF THE LENGTH OF ROPE. IT IS ALSO IMPORTANT THAT THIS PIECE OF ROPE MATCHES THE SKIPPING ROPE AS CLOSELY AS POSSIBLE.

Secret preparation:
The length of rope has to be "gimmicked". Sew the two ends together with the matching thread (Fig. A) to make a loop. You might find it worthwhile to make several

loops as you will destroy one each time you perform the trick. Conceal the gimmicked loop in your hand before you begin.

Take the skipping rope and secretly slide the loop over one of the handles and on to the rope. It is a good idea to check that the loop is big enough to fit over the handles before you start the trick!

Close your hand into a fist around the rope so that the loop is concealed inside. Slide your fist back and forth along the rope and ask one of your audience members to call "Stop" at any point.

When they say "Stop," use your other hand to reach into the top of your fist and pull out part of the loop. This should look to your assembled audience like a section of the rope. Be careful not to pull out too much; otherwise you will reveal that it is a loop – and that will give the game away!

Take the scissors and cut through the piece of rope protuding from your fist. At this point, the owner of the skipping rope will probably protest! Explain that it is okay because you are a magician with special powers and will be able to restore the rope.

When you have cut through the loop, you will be in the position shown in Fig. B. Slide your fingers down to cover the point where the short piece is looped around the skipping rope. It will look as though the rope is really in two pieces!

Turn your hand back into a fist with the cut ends hidden inside and say that you are going to cut the rope again. Very carefully slide the scissors inside the top of the your fist and pretend to cut the rope again. Be very careful not to stab or cut yourself with the scissors!
Remove the scissors and, with your other hand, reach into

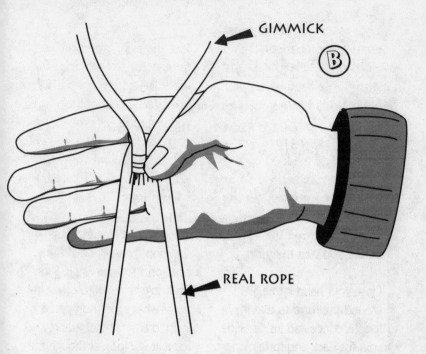

GIMMICK

B

REAL ROPE

the top of your fist and pull out the short piece of rope. Explain that this is a short section that you have cut from the rope! Place the short piece into your pocket. Do not let your audience see it for too long; otherwise they might realise that it does not exactly match the skipping rope.

Now your can remove your fist from around the skipping rope to show that it is completely restored!

TOP TIPS
FOR TRICKSTERS

Your tricks will always have more impact if you 'routine' three or four them together to make a short show.

✦

Have a look at the tricks in this book to see if you can put together your own act.

✦

It is always good to finish with your best trick.

✦

Never get talked into showing more tricks that you haven't rehearsed fully.

✦

Your audience will be more impressed if you do just one or two tricks really well, than several tricks poorly.

PARTY TIME

This chapter is full of
great tricks and
routines for you to
perform at a party, either
as a guest or perhaps as a
paid entertainer!

COIN IN BUN

To the surprise of all the guests around a table, you break open your bread roll and find a coin inside!

Requirements:
A BREAD ROLL AND A COIN.

Secret preparation: Hold the coin in your left hand (Fig. A). If you bend your fingers in slightly, you will discover that they will hold the coin in this position. This is known as the "finger palm". Practise holding a coin like this, so that when you perform the trick you are not worried about it. Your "audience" will only notice the coin if you draw their attention to it with your unnatural actions.

When you are ready to produce the coin from inside a bread roll, pick up

the roll with your right hand and place it into your left hand, so that it covers the palmed coin.

Make a comment about the roll that will gain you the attention of the other guests. Shouting "Watch this!" is good, but not particularly subtle!

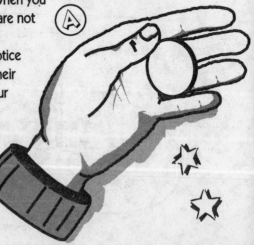

Ⓑ

FIRST,
PARTIALLY
BREAK OPEN THE ROLL
... INSERT COIN ...

Something like "This roll feels very heavy – there must be something inside" is perhaps better.

Slide the roll and the concealed coin up to the left fingertips. Place the left and right thumbs on top of the roll to begin to break it open (Fig. B). At the same time push the coin into the bottom of the roll with the left fingertips. It is important that you get the timing right since you don't want to open the roll and find your fingers inside!

When you open the roll and find the coin inside (Fig. C), smile at your discovery, pocket the money, eat the roll and watch everybody else at the table rip open their rolls looking for change!

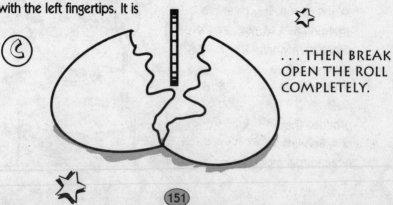

Ⓒ

... THEN BREAK
OPEN THE ROLL
COMPLETELY.

NOSEY SPOON

This is a fun stunt to try at a table, if the situation is right. Don't try it if you're with someone you want to impress!

Requirements:
A METAL SPOON AND YOUR NOSE!

You hang the spoon off the end of your nose (see illustration). Anybody else who tries to do this (and who could resist?) finds that they cannot do it.

There is a secret to this stunt. As you lift up the spoon to balance it on your nose, you breathe heavily into the bowl of the spoon. This creates a small amount of moisture that helps to make the spoon cling.

When you first to do this, you might find it easier if you tilt your head back slightly. Once the spoon is balanced, you can

slowly and gently tilt forwards and, hopefully, the spoon will remain dangling off the end of your nose!

If you want to liven up a dull party, this is the trick to do!

EMIL KIO
1900 - 1965

Kio was a famous Russian
illusionist who frequently
performed with the Moscow
State Circus. He baffled many
magicians by performing many
illusions that are usually
presented on stage, in the centre
of a circus ring, surrounded by
the audience! After his death his
son Igor took over his role.

BENDING SPOON

You can shock your host with this one as you pretend to ruin their cutlery!

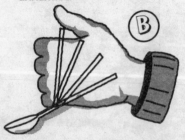

Requirements:
A SPOON AND A TABLE.

Weave together the fingers of both hands to form a "double fist". Hold the spoon so that just a little bit of the top of the handle sticks out above your first fingers and is held in place by pressure of your thumbs. The bowl of the spoon should be sticking out below your little fingers (Fig. A).

Rest the back of the spoon on the table top close to the edge. You are apparently going to press the spoon down on the table top to bend it. In fact, what happens is that you press down and pull your hands slightly back towards you while, at the same time, your thumbs slowly release the tip of the handle. The handle secretly moves down between your hands (which remain upright) and your thumbs stay in position as though they were still holding the tip (Fig. B).

Before the host faints, pull the spoon out of your hands to reveal that it is completely unharmed!

154

TISSUES TO PARTY HAT

You transform torn tissues into a bright tissue-paper party hat!

Requirements:

A TISSUE-PAPER PARTY HAT, TISSUE-PAPER TO MATCH THE HAT, GLUE.

Secret preparation: This is similar to the Torn and Restored Tissues trick that follows. The hat is actually on the back of the tissue paper. However, it is not stuck to the back; it is concealed inside a small pocket, which you make.

To make the pocket, cut a piece of matching tissue that is slightly bigger than the size of the folded hat. Glue three sides of it to the back of one of the sheets of the tissue (Fig. A). When the glue has dried, place the folded hat inside this pocket (Fig. B).

SHEET OF
TISSUE PAPER

FOLDED PARTY
HAT IN HERE

When you perform the trick, remember to keep the pocket side towards you. Tear up the tissue – being careful not to tear through the pocket and the hat.

Bunch up the torn tissue into a small package. Reach into the centre of these torn pieces and remove the hat from its secret pocket. Dispose of the torn pieces as you wonder out loud what it is you have produced. Slowly start to unfold the hat and finally present it to the party boy or girl!

TORN AND RESTORED TISSUES

You can demonstrate your amazing healing powers with this trick by restoring torn tissues and paper napkins.

Requirements:

TWO IDENTICAL PAPER NAPKINS OR TISSUES AND GLUE.

Secret preparation: Fold one of the tissues into a small packet approximately 2 x 2 inches (5 x 5 cm). We will call this packet X. Using a small dab of glue, stick this packet to the back of the other tissue (Fig. A). From the front, this tissue should look okay. Nobody must know about the second tissue stuck to the back.

To perform the trick, show the tissue (remembering not to let anybody see packet X stuck on the back) and tear it up into strips, being careful not to tear at the point where the packet is stuck.

Square all the torn pieces together making sure that the piece connected to packet A goes at the back. Now fold all the torn pieces forwards to make a packet that resembles packet X. You should now have two similar looking packets of tissue stuck back to back – one made up of torn pieces (we

will call this packet Z) and the other (X) a complete piece of tissue paper.

Simply turn the whole thing around so that packet A faces the audience and packet Z faces you. Unfold packet X to show that the torn pieces have joined back together again and are restored (Fig. B)! The real torn pieces (Z) will be hanging on the back hidden from sight!

An important tip to remember with this trick: don't perform it in front of a window or with a strong source of light behind you. If the audience can see through the tissue or napkin it's not a very impressive trick!

THE CHANGING BALLOON

When a pin is stuck into a balloon, instead of bursting as expected, it changes colour!

Requirements:

TWO OPAQUE BALLOONS OF CONTRASTING COLOURS AND A PIN.

Secret preparation: The secret to this trick is that both balloons are blown up, one inside the other, and it is the outer balloon that is burst. The toughest part of this trick is the preparation – getting one uninflated balloon inside the other, blowing them up so that the outer balloon is just a little bit larger and knotting the necks of both balloons

together. The first time you do this may be a bit of a struggle. It will take a little while to develop the knack, but once you've done it you'll feel great! The secret to this is to inflate the balloon about half way before placing the inner balloon inside and inflating that so that they both expand.

To perform the trick, show the balloon and explain to your audience that it is a magic balloon, because when you prick it with a needle, instead of popping, something magical happens. Display the pin and bring it close to the balloon. Tell the audience that they can put their fingers in their ears if they don't trust you. The chances are they will all put their fingers in their ears. At this point, you could make a joke about them not trusting you!

Prick the outer balloon with the pin and it will pop revealing the contrasting coloured balloon inside (see illustration). To your audience, it will appear as though the balloon has magically changed colour!

BOUNCING BUN

This is another fun stunt for the party table, in which you throw a bread roll on the floor and it bounces back up, as though made of rubber.

Requirements:

A BREAD ROLL.

Hold a bread roll in your right hand and move your right arm and hand down below the edge of the table as though you are throwing the roll at the floor. In fact, you never let go of the roll. Figs A and B show what secretly happens when your hand gets below the edge of the table. Your hand turns palm up and throws the roll up as though it has bounced off

the floor (Fig. C).

There are a number of things that can make this stunt even more effective. First, it is important that only your hand moves when you throw the roll upwards. Your arm must remain rigid; it must not give away the fact that your hand is moving.

Second, you can create the

noise of the roll hitting the floor by stamping the heel of one of your shoes on the floor. This is only effective if you do it at the moment when the roll would be bouncing.

And third, and most importantly, timing is the most important part of this stunt. Although it may appear to be just an impromptu gag at the party table, as with everything in this book it should be rehearsed to perfection before you attempt to show it to anybody. And the thing that must be perfect for this stunt to work is the timing. If the stamp of your foot or the upward throw is not correct, everybody will sense that it was a trick. When it is done well, it looks amazing. Just make sure that it *is* amazing when you do it!

STAMP ALBUM

A collection of stamps vanishes from a bag and fills the pages of a previously empty stamp album!

Requirements:

A LARGE COLLECTION OF STAMPS (YOU CAN BUY BULK QUANTITIES OF STAMPS FROM COLLECTING SHOPS AND MAGAZINES), A STAMP ALBUM, SCISSORS AND A "MAGIC MARBLE BAG" (SEE P. 136).

Secret preparation: This trick relies on two special props that you have already seen in this book: the "Magic Marble Bag" and the long and short exercise book featured in "Homework by Magic" (see p. 104). As with that exercise book, cut every other page of the stamp album a little bit short. When you have done this, stick

stamps into the album on every other two-page spread (making sure that you are left with some spare ones). When this is completed, you will find (as before) that, when you flick through the book one way, it will appear empty, and when you flick the other way, it will appear full.

BLANK

Ⓐ

To get ready for your performance, place the spare loose stamps into one side of the marble bag and have the album nearby.

STAMPS!

Ⓑ

Ask your audience how many of them collect stamps. Tell them that you collect stamps too, but you always forget to stick them into your album. Flick through the album to show that it is empty (Fig. A).

Invite someone to help you stick in the stamps by magic. Ask them to cup their hands together and then tip the stamps out of the bag and into their hands. You can create a funny situation by "accidently" knocking the stamps on to the floor. Put the stamps back

into one side of the bag and ask your audience to call out the magic word.

Turn the empty side of the bag inside out – it appears as though all the stamps have vanished. Now flick through the book to reveal that the stamps have appeared inside and stuck themselves in by magic (Fig. B). Thank your helper and take your bow!

AFGHAN BANDS CONTEST

This comic competition is a classic of children's magic and will provide an entertaining few minutes of fun at any party.

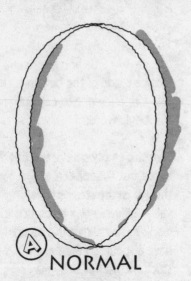

(A) NORMAL

Secret preparation: You need to make three large loops by sticking together the ends of each of the strips of the paper. However, two of the loops (B and C) are specially prepared (see illustration). Before sticking together the ends of strip B, put a single twist in the paper, and before sticking together the ends of strip C, put in a double twist. Mark the loops A, B and C so that you know which is which!

Requirements:
THREE STRIPS OF PAPER APPROXIMATELY 4 FEET (1.2 M) LONG AND 2 INCHES (5 CM) WIDE, THREE PAIRS OF SCISSORS AND GLUE.

Invite two people to participate in the competition – one boy and one girl. You can have fun by asking all the boys to cheer for the boy and all the girls to cheer for the girl.

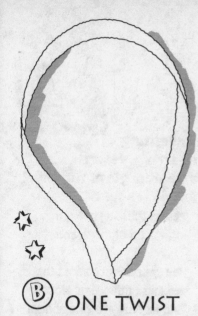

Ⓑ ONE TWIST

Hand the boy loop B and the girl loop C; also give each a pair of scissors.

Using strip A to demonstrate, explain that the idea of the competition is to cut along the middle of the length of the paper strip until you are left with two separate loops. Point out that they have to be careful not to snip too close to the edge; otherwise they might ruin their chances!

To make it even tougher, tell them that it is a race, with a prize for the first to finish.

Then: "On your marks, get set, go!" The boy and girl now rush to cut along the middle of their loops to cheers of encouragement from the audience.

However, when they have both finished, they are both disqualified because the boy only has one giant loop and the girl's loops are joined together! In the end, you decide it is a tie and give them both a prize!

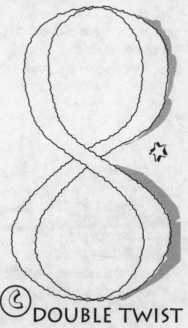

ⒸDOUBLE TWIST

HOUDINI SILK

A silk handkerchief, representing the world famous escape artiste Harry Houdini, escapes from a sealed glass tumbler!

Requirements:

TWO DIFFERENT-COLOURED SILK HANDKERCHIEFS, A LARGE SILK SCARF, 10 INCHES (25 CM) OF COTTON THREAD, A GLASS TUMBLER AND AN ELASTIC BAND.

Secret preparation: Tie one end of the length of thread on to one corner of the handkerchief that you want to

"escape". Tie a knot in the other end of the thread.

Tell the audience about the exploits of the Great Houdini and his ability to escape from any confinement – prison cells, packing cases, straitjackets and handcuffs. Explain that your audience is very fortunate because, for the first time ever, you are going to introduce the reincarnation of Houdini – as a handkerchief!

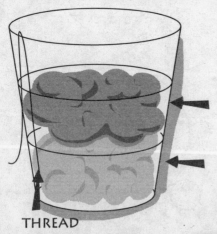

(A)

"PRISON GUARD" SILK

"HOUDINI" SILK

THREAD

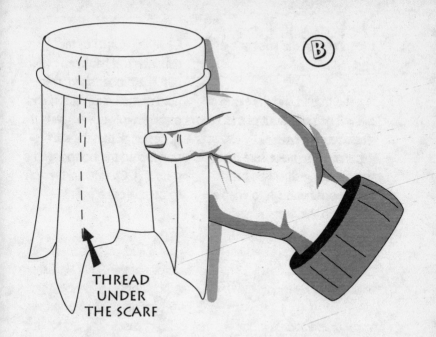

(B)

THREAD
UNDER
THE SCARF

Display the "Houdini handkerchief" and push it down into the bottom of the empty tumbler. As you do this, make sure that the thread is hanging outside of the glass.

Introduce the second handkerchief as a prison guard and stuff it into the tumbler on top of the first handkerchief (Fig. A).

To make extra sure that the handkerchief is unable to escape, throw the scarf over the mouth of the tumbler and hold it in place with the elastic band (Fig. B). You could call this the padded cell . . . or perhaps that is taking the story a bit too far!

Now jokingly tell the audience that this escape used to take 30 minutes, but today you intend to double that time! After suitable build-up of tension, reach up under the scarf and take hold of the thread by the knot at the end.

Pull the thread and the Houdini silk will be pulled out of the glass. You will have to experiment to make sure that you are using an elastic band that is loose enough to enable you to do this.

Once the corner of the handkerchief has been pulled past the rubber band, grab hold of the handkerchief and pull it sharply down, giving the appearance that the silk has penetrated the bottom of the glass (Fig. C). Houdini lives on to escape once again!

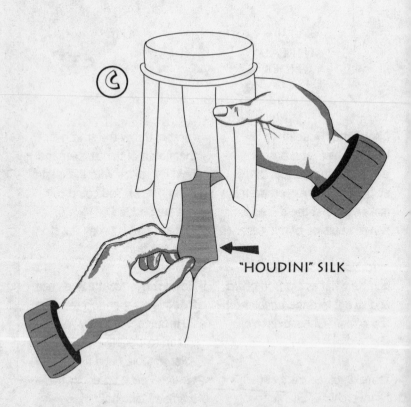

"HOUDINI" SILK

TOP TIPS FOR TRICKSTERS USING SILK HANDKERCHIEFS

If you are using silk handkerchiefs in your performances you can prevent them from becoming frayed at the edges by double-hemming them. Fold over the original hem and sew them again.

✧

A good way to prevent silk handkerchiefs looking creased is to wash them while they are screwed up very tight. This will make them almost "crease proof".

✧

Always have an emergency sewing kit in your "bag of tricks" when you have any hanky tricks in the act!

SHIRT OFF THE BACK

This is a great stunt for a party. You will surprise and amaze all the guests when you rip off the shirt of one of them without first removing their jacket!

Requirements:

A FRIEND WITH A SHIRT AND JACKET.

Secret preparation: The secret is that it is your friend whose shirt you remove. If there are strangers at the party you and your friend should pretend not to know each other, it makes the shock even greater when you rip off his shirt.

Before the party, help your friend put on the shirt in a special way (*see illustration*). First, do up the top few buttons, but leave the shirt hanging down his back. Put the sleeves down the outside of his arms and do up the cuff buttons. Help him on with his jacket which he buttons. Make sure that, from the front, it looks as though the shirt is on properly and that the shirt cuffs stick out of his jacket sleeves. You are now ready to amaze the party guests.

At the party, explain that you will try to remove his shirt without undoing his jacket. Ask him to sit down in front of you. Undo his shirt front and cuff buttons. Grab hold of his shirt collar and pull it upwards.

(170)

Continue pulling until you have pulled the shirt off and your friend is left wearing only his jacket!

DAVID COPPERFIELD

The American illusionist, David Copperfield, is well known for his own television specials and spectacular stunts. In just over a decade he has vanished a Lear Jet, the Statue of Liberty and a coach from the Orient Express! He has walked through the Great Wall of China, vanished in the Bermuda Triangle and survived going over Niagara Falls! He began by performing at children's parties as the "Great Davido" and appeared on his first TV show soon after playing the starring role in the musical "The Magic Man". He tours around the world with his live pop-concert style show, during which he has been known to fly on stage or cause the arena to fill with snow!

CUT AND RESTORED RIBBON

After cutting through a bright ribbon – perhaps to open a party or fair – you magically turn it back into one piece!

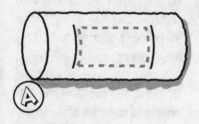

Requirements:
A LENGTH OF RIBBON, AN ENVELOPE, SCISSORS AND TAPE.

Secret preparation: You need to "gimmick" the envelope for this trick. First, seal it and cut off the two short ends to make a flat tube. Now cut two slits in the back of the envelope, parallel to the short ends (Fig. A). Finally cut a short piece of ribbon and tape this

to the inside of the envelope between the two slits (Fig. B), with the tape being placed on the ends near the slits.

Set this envelope on your table with the secret slits at the back, and have the scissors and length of ribbon nearby. You are now set to perform the trick.

Display the ribbon and push one end into the envelope as if you are going to push the ribbon through it. In fact, by

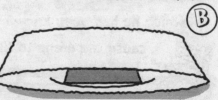

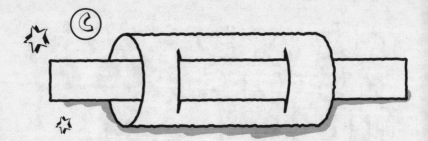

bowing the envelope, the ribbon goes through the slits and passes through the back of the envelope (Fig. C). Remember to keep this back view of the envelope completely hidden from your audience.

Open the scissors and slide one blade between the ribbon and the back of the envelope (Fig. D) so that, when you cut the envelope in half, the ribbon is not cut.

Cut the envelope. Fold it in half (folding the ribbon in

half, too), so you can show the cut ends of the ribbon inside. (Of course this is just the small section of ribbon that you had secretly stuck inside, but to the audience, it appears to be the long ribbon.)

Hold the two halves of the cut envelope together and pull on one of the long ends of the ribbon – or, better still, ask an audience member to pull. The ribbon will emerge from the envelope completely unharmed. Get rid of the gimmicked envelope as soon as possible!

THE PROFESSOR'S NIGHTMARE

You stretch three pieces of rope – all of different lengths – between your hands and they all become the same length! The ropes are tied together, but still return to their original sizes. This effect is sometimes known as the "Equal Unequal Ropes".

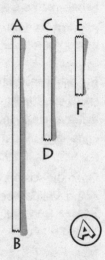

Requirements:

THREE PIECES OF ROPE – APPROXIMATELY 24 INCHES (60 CM), 12 INCHES (30 CM) AND 8 INCHES (20 CM) LONG. IT IS IMPORTANT THAT ALL THREE PIECES ARE THE SAME COLOUR. YOU WILL SEE WHY IN A MOMENT.

Let the audience examine the three lengths of rope. Ask them to make sure that the ropes do not stretch. Collect the ropes from the audience.

You must clip one end of each length of rope between your left thumb and index finger. The order of the ropes must be as in Fig. A, so that the longest rope (AB) is nearest the thumb crotch.

With your right hand, bring end B up to your left hand, so that it is clipped by the left thumb

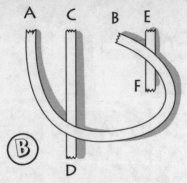

between ends C and E. Make sure that the rope passes over the top of rope EF (Fig. B).

The right hand brings up ends F and D into the left hand, so that they are to the right of the ends being clipped. You will see from Fig. C that the above procedure results in ropes AB and EF being looped together. This prepares you for the "big stretch"!

Take ends A, C and B in your left hand and E, F and D in your

right hand and slowly pull your hands apart. Amazingly it will appear that the three ropes stretch between your hands to become the same length. It is important that your right hand stays closed around the point where the short and long ropes are linked.

This puts you in the position shown in Fig. D. To convince the audience that the three ropes really are of the same length, you now perform a special false count. It appears that you count the ropes singly from hand to hand, but in fact, you conceal the fact that two of them are looped together. Here's what really happens . . .

The right hand takes the

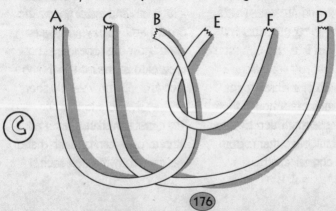

medium-length rope (CD) from the left hand and moves to the right as you say, "One." The right hand moves back and puts the medium length into the left thumb crotch as the right second and third fingers grasp the looped short and long ropes and move them to the right as you say, "Two." On the count of "Three," the right hand removes the medium length of rope (CD) from the left hand.

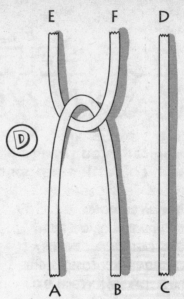

Let go of ends A, B and C with your left hand, and tie ends EF into a knot around rope AB. It should appear that you are just tying two ends of rope together, but in reality you are tying the short piece around the long piece to make a sliding knot.

When the knot is tight and is not going to slip off the rope, let go and tie end B to end C. It should appear that you are making a long length of all three ropes. Explain that, even though the ropes are securely tied together, you can still make them return to their original lengths.

Wrap the ropes around your left hand. As you slide the rope around your hand, slide the knot at the same time. Secretly move the knot until it is at one end of the long rope it is tied around.

Show the ropes coiled around your hand, snap your fingers and show the ropes have now returned to their original lengths. You now have a short piece, tied to a long piece, tied to a medium-sized piece. All three ropes can be untied and examined by the audience.

CONFETTI-TO-CANDY CUP

Magically you change a cup filled with confetti into popcorn.

Requirements:

TWO IDENTICAL OPAQUE PARTY CUPS, CARDBOARD, CONFETTI, A CARDBOARD BOX, SCISSORS, GLUE, PAPER NAPKINS, POPCORN AND A GLASS TUMBLER.

Secret preparation: First of all, you need to make a special gimmick. Trace around the mouth of one of the cups on to the cardboard and cut out the circle, making it just slightly smaller than the circumference of the cup mouth. On to this cardboard disc, glue some

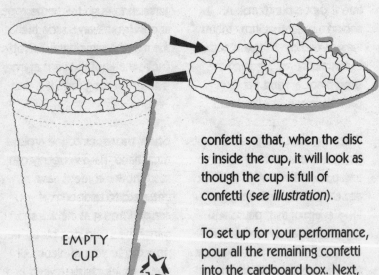

EMPTY CUP

confetti so that, when the disc is inside the cup, it will look as though the cup is full of confetti (*see illustration*).

To set up for your performance, pour all the remaining confetti into the cardboard box. Next, half-fill one of the cups with popcorn. Place the gimmicked disc into the mouth of the cup so that the popcorn is hidden and the cup looks as though it is full of confetti. Place this cup inside the box on top of the confetti. Make sure that the box is positioned so that your audience cannot see the cup inside the box. Have the other empty cup on hand nearby, with the paper napkins and glass tumbler.

Explain to your audience that you are going to show them how it is possible to make popcorn by magic. Show them the empty cup. With your empty hand, reach into the cardboard box and bring out a handful of confetti. Explain that you are going to use confetti as your special ingredient. Dip the empty cup into the box and scoop up some confetti until the cup is about half full. Bring out the cup again, then pause and say, "No, I need more than that."

Dip the cup back into the box, but this time leave it behind in the box and bring out the other cup. It should look as though you have filled up the cup with confetti. Nobody should be suspicious of the cup – unless you have made them suspicious! So don't!

Cover the mouth of the cup with paper napkins and ask your audience to shout out some magic words. Using your fingers, push down through the napkin on to one side of the disc, which will pivot inside the top of the cup. Grab the gimmick through the napkin and whisk it away to reveal that the magic has happened! Drop the napkin into the cardboard box (with the gimmick).

Tip the popcorn out of the paper cup and into the glass tumbler so that everybody can see that the confetti has changed into popcorn. If you are performing at a children's party, you could distribute the popcorn to your audience or give it to the children who assist you in your show.

SQUARED CIRCLE PRODUCTION BOX

You show two square tubes to be completely empty. It appears that nothing can be concealed inside. And yet you reach inside and produce a large number of silk handkerchiefs, ribbons, and maybe the props for your next effect!

Requirements:

TWO SQUARE TUBES THAT NEST ONE INSIDE THE OTHER, A SMALL BOX THAT WILL FIT INSIDE THE NESTED TUBES, SILK HANDKER-CHIEFS, RIBBONS AND ANYTHING ELSE THAT YOU WISH TO PRODUCE.

Secret preparation: Cut a small hole in the front of the larger tube. Paint the small box and the interior of both tubes with a matt black paint. Cover the outside of the two tubes with a bright design. Fill the black box with the items that you want to produce. Depending on the size of this production box, you could produce sweets or full glasses for your audience, maybe even soft toys or pets!

Load the black box inside the two nested tubes. Place this on your table, with the hole in the larger, outer tube facing the audience.

Remove the outer tube and hold it up before the audience to show it is empty. Place it back in position around the inner tube.

Lift up the inner tube. This, too, is held up and shown to be empty. The audience can also see through the hole in the large tube. However, because the production box has been painted black, they will believe that they are seeing the back of the outer tube. This clever principle is known among magicians as "black art".

Replace the inner tube back inside the larger tube. After sufficient build-up, roll up your sleeves, show that both your hands are empty and make your production from your own "Pandora's Box".

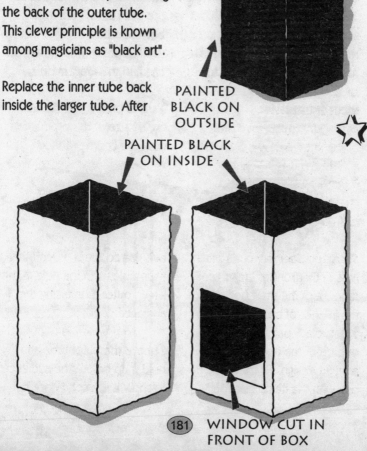

PAINTED
BLACK ON
OUTSIDE

PAINTED BLACK
ON INSIDE

WINDOW CUT IN
FRONT OF BOX

MAGIC WASHING

You securely tie handkerchiefs on to two ropes held between two volunteers. The handkerchiefs magically penetrate through the ropes.

Requirements:

TWO IDENTICAL LENGTHS OF ROPE APPROXIMATELY 4 FEET (1.2 M) LONG, AT LEAST FOUR CLEAN HANDKERCHIEFS (PREFERABLY SILK), AND A MAGIC WAND (ANY PIECE OF DOWEL PAINTED BLACK WITH WHITE ENDS!).

Invite two members of your audience to assist you. Stretch the two ropes, held together, between them. Explain that you are doing this so that you can find the exact middle.

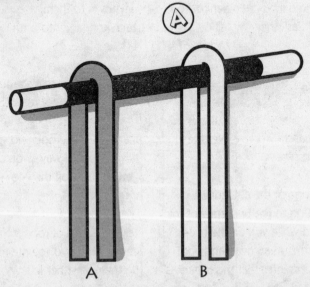

(A)

A   B

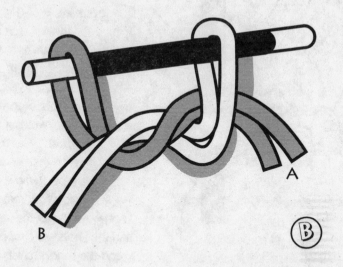

A

B

Hold the wand under the ropes. If there are young children in your audience, you could ask them to call out "Stop!" when you reach the middle of the ropes. When the wand is held under the middle of the ropes, ask your volunteers to release the ends so that they drape over the wand (Fig. A).

Ask one of the audience to hold on to the two ends of the wand while you tie the ropes together in an overhand knot (it is essential that this is tied as

in Fig. B). Hand two ends back to each of your volunteers. Unknown to them, they are each holding onto both ends of one rope!

Tie the handkerchiefs around the two lengths of rope (Fig. C). Explain that this is your magic washing rope and you have a special way of quickly getting them off the line when it rains.

Take one end of rope from each of the two volunteers and tie them together in an

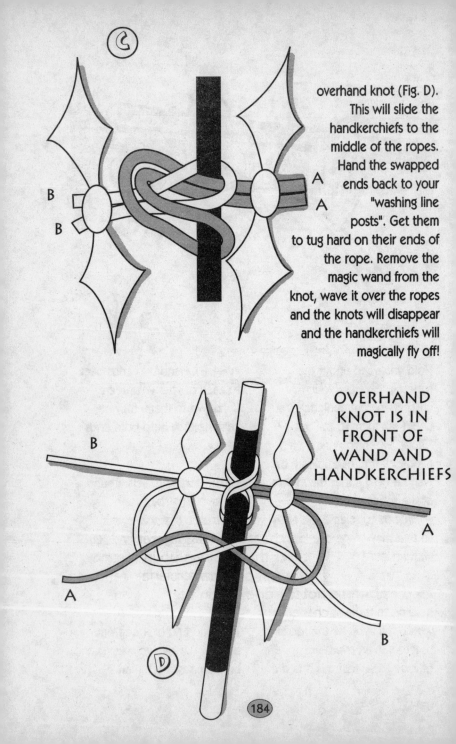

overhand knot (Fig. D). This will slide the handkerchiefs to the middle of the ropes. Hand the swapped ends back to your "washing line posts". Get them to tug hard on their ends of the rope. Remove the magic wand from the knot, wave it over the ropes and the knots will disappear and the handkerchiefs will magically fly off!

OVERHAND KNOT IS IN FRONT OF WAND AND HANDKERCHIEFS

TRICKS ON HOLIDAY

This chapter is full of great tricks that you can do in the car, on a train, plane, in a hotel – or even on the beach!

HIGHWAY MIND READING

On a long journey, you and a friend amaze everyone with your psychic abilities.

Requirements:

ALL YOU NEED IS PAPER, A PEN AND A FRIEND WHO KNOWS THE SECRET!

It seems as though, whenever you just think of a number or letter, your friend knows what it is. That is what the other people travelling with you will think – but then they don't know the secret.

In fact, before the journey you told your friend the special code, which is "red cars". I'd better explain! After saying that you are going to think of a number, look out for the next red car coming towards you on the other side of the road, and remember the first number on the licence plate. For example,

if the car number is "E895 JLD", you would think "8". Your friend, who is also looking out for red cars, sees the number and writes down "8" on the pad. You announce that you are thinking of 8 and your friend shows that he wrote down the correct number.

After you have repeated this a few times, explain that you will make it much harder. You will go from a choice of 9 digits to 26 different letters – very tough!

It's not tough at all really – it is exactly the same! You still look for red cars, only now you always use the last letter. For example, in "E895 JLD", you use "D".

Now you only need to think of something to say when people ask you to display your psychic powers when you are not in a car!

TRICKS YOU CAN BUY

3. THE BOSTON BOX

A special brass box, like the Okito Box; but capable of a lot more.

4. DYNAMIC COINS

You can make a stack of coins appear and disappear from underneath brass caps.

BAFFLING BLINDFOLD

This is a great trick that you can do with one of those blindfolds you get on airplanes to help you sleep and hide from the in-flight movie!

Requirements:

A BLINDFOLD, A SHEET OF PAPER, A PEN AND AN OPAQUE BAG (AN EMPTY AIRLINE SICK BAG IS IDEAL!)

Tear up the piece of paper into nine pieces (*see illustration*) and secretly sort them into those with two torn edges (four pieces), three torn edges (four pieces) and four torn edges (one piece). Nobody should realise that you are sorting the pieces; it should just look as though you are collecting them together.

On each of the two torn-edge pieces, write a word related to holidays (e.g. PLANE, BEACH, SUN, etc.). On each of the three torn-edge pieces, write a

word related to school (e.g. HOMEWORK, RULER, TEACHER, CLASSROOM, etc.). Leave the four torn-edge piece blank. Drop all nine pieces into the bag and ask a friend to shake them up.

Explain that, even though the bag has been shaken and the pieces mixed up, you are going to reach inside and be able to tell them the category of word with your fingertips! And, to make sure you don't peek into the bag, you blindfold yourself!

Reach inside the bag and pick up one of the pieces. Of course, you don't read it with your fingertips, but you can feel the edges! If the paper has two torn edges, the word relates to holidays; if it has three torn edges, the word relates to school; and if it has four torn edges, it is blank. Announce which category the word is and remove your hand from the bag to show your "audience" that you are correct.

When you have correctly "read" all the pieces of paper, you can dramatically whip off your blindfold and take your applause from your fellow passengers!

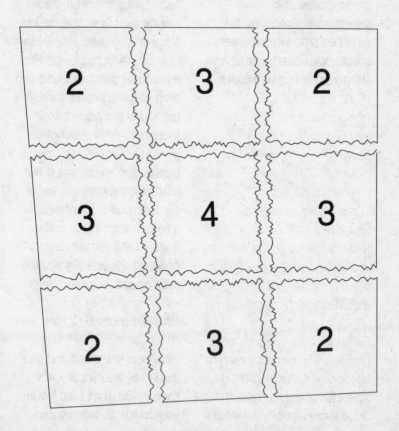

TICKETS PLEASE

You can amaze the ticket inspector – and your travelling companions – by causing your train ticket to rise mysteriously from your pocket!

Requirements:

A VALID TICKET (OBVIOUSLY!), A JACKET OR SHIRT WITH AN EMPTY OUTSIDE TOP POCKET, A NEEDLE AND THREAD THAT MATCHES THE JACKET OR SHIRT.

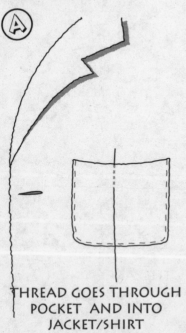

THREAD GOES THROUGH POCKET AND INTO JACKET/SHIRT

Secret preparation: This does require a bit of setting up, but it is worth the effort to see the look on everybody's faces! You need to thread the needle and then stick the needle through the top of the pocket and then through the front of the jacket or shirt (Fig. A). Leave enough thread hanging down at the front so you can easily grab the end in your hand. Tie a knot in the thread on the inside of the garment and break off the rest (Fig. B). You are now set.

On the day of travel, wear your special shirt or jacket, and when you get your ticket, push it carefully into the prepared top pocket so that the bottom edge of the ticket pushes

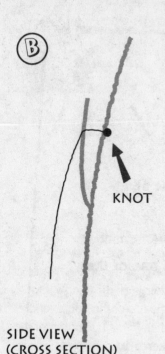

(B)

with your left hand and watch your ticket magically and mysteriously rise out of your pocket!

KNOT

SIDE VIEW
(CROSS SECTION)

down the thread passing across the top of the pocket (Fig. C).

When you see the inspector coming towards you, grab the end of the thread in your left hand ready to make the magic happen. When you are asked for your ticket, just look down at your pocket and, when everybody is looking at it, too, pull on the end of the thread

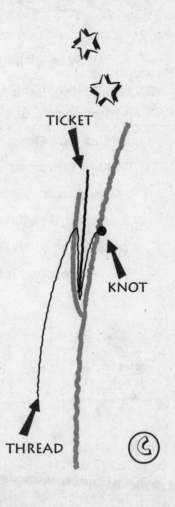

TICKET

KNOT

THREAD

(C)

ADE DUVAL

Many magicians use silk
handkerchiefs in their
performances, but the American
magician Ade Duval was one of the
few to create an entire act of
'Silken Sorcery'. With this unique
act, he travelled the world
performing in all the exclusive,
glamorous night spots.

BALL AND BUCKETS

On the beach, you use your X-ray vision to reveal which bucket has a beachball underneath!

Requirements:

THREE BUCKETS, A BEACHBALL (WHICH WILL FIT WITHIN ANY OF THE BUCKETS) AND A LONG HAIR.

Secret preparation: This actually has nothing to do with X-ray vision! Before you get to the beach, obtain a long hair from someone and attach it to the beachball. Most beachballs have plastic nozzles where they have been blown up, and you should be able to tie the hair on to that. Now you are set to hit the beach!

Ask a friend to hide the ball under one of the three buckets while you look away. When you turn around, you are instantly able to tell your friend which bucket the ball is under!

The secret is simple – you just look to see which bucket the hair is sticking out of and that tells you the ball is underneath (*see illustration*)! Nobody else will notice the hair attached to the ball; in the bright sunshine, it will be almost invisible.

SLEIGHT OF BEACHBALL

This is a card trick for the beach. You kick a beachball at the pack and it cuts at the selected card!

Requirements:

A BEACHBALL AND A PACK OF CARDS

This is a trick that will only work on a sandy beach. You'll soon see why!

Ask someone to choose a card from the pack, look at it, remember it and put it back on top of the pack. Now you need to put the pack a short distance away so you can kick the beachball at it.

As you move the pack, "accidently" get sand on top of it – not too much, just a few grains. When you have done this, cut the pack and put it back together so that the card is apparently lost in the middle of the pack (Fig.A). I say "apparently" because the card has a few grains of sand on top of it! Now you know why you have to do this trick on a sandy beach!

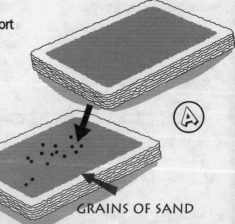

GRAINS OF SAND

Put the pack down on the sand and knock the beachball towards it. Don't kick the ball too hard – you're not trying to score a goal! You simply want to knock the pack so that the grains of sand in the middle of it act like miniature ball bearings and cause the pack to split at that point (Fig.B).

Now you can turn over the card at the point where the pack cut – it will be the selected card!

You can do a version of this trick away from the beach, using grains of salt instead of sand. Perhaps you could accidently knock a salt cellar on to the pack at a dinner table? Perhaps you won't get invited to dinner again!

CARD-IN-SAND PREDICTION

A prediction of a selected playing card, buried in the sand on the beach, proves to be correct!

Requirements:

A PACK OF CARDS AND ONE EXTRA PREDICTION CARD.

Secret preparation: Bury the prediction card (let's assume that it is the four of diamonds) just below the surface of the sand, so that it can be removed easily. (You don't want to spend 20 minutes trying to find it!) Place the regular card that matches the prediction (in our example, the four of diamonds)

on top of the pack.

You've probably guessed that you're going to "force" the four of diamonds. You could use the "Cards under the Handkerchief" force, which I explained in The Mindreading Banana (see p. 75). However, you might prefer the "Slip Cut" force.

Hold the pack so that your fingertips are touching the back of the top card (Fig. A). Place your left thumb on the top left-hand corner of the top card of the pack and riffle it down the pack (Fig. B), releasing the cards

(196)

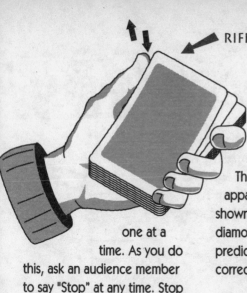

RIFFLE

one at a time. As you do this, ask an audience member to say "Stop" at any time. Stop flicking when "Stop" is called.

Your right hand is now, apparently, going to take away all the cards above the point at which you have stopped. In fact, what happens is that the right hand holds these cards by the short edges – the thumb at one end, fingers at the other – and pulls them up. And, at the same time, the left fingertips press on the top card – the force card – holding it in position and secretly slipping it on to the top of the bottom half of the pack (Fig. C). This is

why it is called the "Slip Cut" force.

The card that you apparently stopped at is shown to be the four of diamonds. When your prediction card is revealed, it is correct!

Of course, you can use this force for other tricks. How many other ways to reveal a prediction can you think of? You could write the name of the card in the sand, or in suntan lotion on your back!

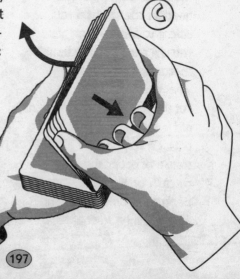

(C)

DRY SAND

On the beach, you can amaze everybody by reaching into a bucket in which you have mixed sand and seawater and removing a handful of perfectly dry sand!

Requirements:

BUCKET, SAND, WAX CANDLE AND AN OLD FRYING PAN! (THIS IS STARTING TO SOUND LIKE A RECIPE!)

Secret preparation: It's not as simple as it sounds – in fact, this is probably the toughest trick in the book to prepare! You will need an adult to help you. Before you even go on holiday, you will need to make some special "waterproof sand".

Put some fine, dry sand into an old frying pan and heat it up until it is very hot. Cut a little square of paper and drop it carefully on the sand: when the paper turns brown, the sand is hot enough! Add about 3/4 inch (2 cm) of ordinary white wax candle (*see illustration*). When the wax has melted, stir it into the sand.

Turn off the heat and let the sand get completely cold. It will come out of the pan in one solid lump, which you can crumble up to look like regular sand again. But now it is waterproof sand and this is what you take to the beach.

On the beach, you can mix this specially prepared sand with seawater – or even with regular tap water – and when you scoop it out, it will be dry!

VANISHING WATER

This is fun to do at the beach or at a swimming pool closer to home! You can pour water into a bucket or mug, but when you turn it upside down, not a drop falls out – it has vanished!

Requirements:

AN OPAQUE CONTAINER (A MUG OR BUCKET), SOME WATER AND A SPONGE.

Special preparation: The sponge is the secret behind this one! It is stuck in the bottom of the container and soaks up the liquid that is poured inside! To prepare, secretly jam a sponge in the bottom of the container (*see illustration*). Make sure you rehearse this before showing anybody so that you know how much water the sponge will safely absorb! Also make sure that the sponge does not fall out, since it will be much heavier when it has soaked up the water!

SPONGE WEDGED IN BOTTOM OF BUCKET

Pour the liquid into the container and say the magic words (this gives time for the water to become absorbed into the sponge). Now you can turn the cup or bucket upside down without a drop falling out!

In a restaurant, you could secretly put ice cubes inside the mug with the sponge, before adding the water. When you turn the mug over, the ice cubes will fall out and it will look as though you have turned water into ice!

LIGHT CONTROL

You can amaze your fellow passengers in a car by making traffic lights change to green!

The secret to this is actually very simple, but it is amazing how many people you can fool with it.

This will only work at a crossroads or anywhere where there are traffic lights causing traffic to stop so that you can go. All you have to do is watch the other traffic (*see illustration*), because there will be a few seconds between their lights changing to red and your lights changing to green. So, as soon as the traffic in the other direction stops moving, shout at your lights, "Change to green!" – and they will, as if completely under your control!

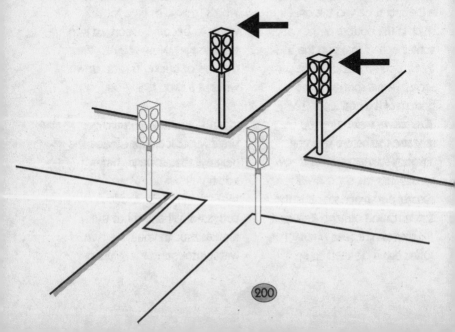

CUT AND RESTORED HEADPHONES

On a plane, you can shock your fellow passengers and airline attendant by cutting and restoring the headphones provided.

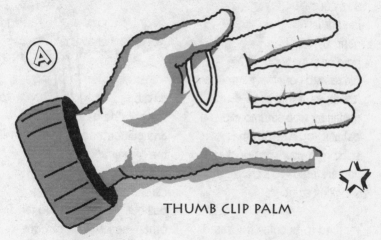

(A)

THUMB CLIP PALM

Requirements:
A PAIR OF SCISSORS AND THE AIRLINE HEADPHONES.

Secret preparation: This is similar to the Cut and Restored Skipping Rope (see p. 145). Once again, you will need to make a special secret gimmick. However, this time it is easy because the airline provides it for you!

You need to hang on to the black plastic tie that is wrapped around the wires of the headphones when you are given them. This small piece of black plastic looks almost identical to the black wires of the headphones and is what you are going to cut through! Fold the piece of wire in half and conceal it in your left hand by holding it in place with your left thumb (known to magicians as a "thumb clip palm") (Fig. A). With the scissors in your right pocket, you are ready to perform this shocking stunt.

Pretend to become frustrated with the in-flight movie or radio channels. Eventually decide you have had enough. Disconnect the headphones from the socket in the armrest. Make a fist around the headphone wire with the fingers of your left hand, and with your right fingers and

thumb, reach inside and pull out the "gimmick" (Fig. B). Be careful not to pull out the gimmick too far; otherwise it will be obvious that it is not connected. To your "audience" – your fellow passengers – this will look like the actual cable.

Reach into your pocket with your right hand and remove the scissors. Cut through the gimmick. It appears as though you have cut through the cable and destroyed the headphones!

Very carefully slide the scissors inside the top of the your fist and pretend to cut the cable again. Be very careful not to stab or cut yourself with the scissors!

Replace the scissors in your pocket and then reach into the top of your fist and pull out the short piece of wire. Explain that this is a short section that you have cut from the cable because there was interference! Place the short piece into your pocket. Do not let your audience see it for too long; they might realise that it does not exactly match the cable.

After saying some appropriate magic words, open your left hand so that your audience can see that the cable is restored. Plug your headphones back in and say you are delighted because the interference has gone!

You could present this stunt in a different way by pretending to get angry with the noise coming from a passenger's headphones and finally cut through them to stop the noise! Of course, to do this, make sure that you know the person before you approach them waving a pair of scissors around. Some people don't like this!

And, of course, I don't have to remind you never to cut through live electrical cables!

SUNGLASSES THRU NECK

On holiday, you can amaze your friends by pulling your sunglasses' cord right through your neck!

Requirements:

A PAIR OF SUNGLASSES, THE ARMS OF WHICH ARE ATTACHED TO A CORD SO THAT YOU CAN HANG THEM AROUND YOUR NECK. YOU MUST ALSO BE WEARING A T-SHIRT OR COLLARED SHIRT TO PERFORM THIS.

Secret preparation: In fact, the cord goes around the front of your neck and not the back as people will assume. This is why you must be wearing a shirt as this will hide the cord at the front. The illustration shows exactly where the cord is hidden. When you have set up the cord like this, you will be ready to remove your sunglasses in a dramatic and magical fashion!

To perform this, lift your sunglasses up a little way so that they are off your ears. Unhook the cord from behind your ears and then dramatically pull your sunglasses forwards. The cord will be pulled out of the front of your shirt and will appear as though it has been pulled right through your neck!

HOW TO MAKE ANY NATIONAL MONUMENT VANISH

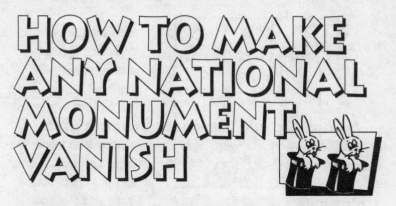

Yes, just like those spectacular TV magicians you will now be able to make any large national monument – the Statue of Liberty, the Eiffel Tower, Big Ben, anything – vanish!

Requirements:
POSTCARDS OR PHOTOGRAPHS, A RUBBER BAND AND SCISSORS.

Secret preparation: You are going to use the principle behind the 'Out to Lunch' trick (see p. 138) to make any large national monument vanish from a photograph. You will need a photograph or postcard of the monument, in which the monument only appears in the top half (picture 1, Fig. A). You

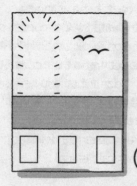

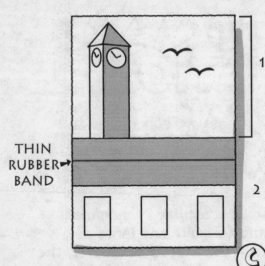

THIN
RUBBER →
BAND

Hold the stack of postcards with the picture pointing up. **1** Point out to your friends the national monument. Turn the stack of postcards so that the picture is pointing down and pull out picture 2. **2** Make sure that you pull out the card from the correct end; otherwise you will pull out the half card – and that gives the trick away!

also need a photograph or postcard of an identical setting that doesn't include the monument (picture 2, Fig. B).

Make a stack of postcards or photographs with picture 2 on top and place the rubber band around the stack. Now cut picture 1 in half and place the half featuring the monument on top of picture 2. Hold it in position with the rubber band (Fig. C). It should look like a single picture. Now you are all set to start.

When you pull out the picture, the rubber band will hold the half card in position. Keeping the stack facing down, get rid of it (be careful not to let anybody see the half card still under the rubber band). Keep the picture card facing down and make a magical pass over it. When the card is turned over, the monument has vanished!

IT'S SHOWTIME

All

This chapter features some classic tricks that are ideal for stage performances. It even includes a couple of spectacular illusions you can do!

But first, I want to give you some idea about how to put on a show – either at home, at school or at a children's party.

THE MAGIC WAND

If you want to put together an act or an entire show, your first essential magicians' accessory is a magic wand. The wand has been used by magicians for many centuries as a symbol of their power. However, you can make one from a piece of dowelling!

You need a piece of dowelling about 14 inches (35 cm) long and 1/2 inch (1.2 cm) thick. Sand it down with sandpaper and give it an undercoat of paint. When it is dry, paint the ends white and the rest of it black.

In addition to waving your wand during the tricks apparently to make the magic happen, there are a few tricks that show off the magic wand's powers.

You could use it instead of a pen in the Uri Geller Pen (p. 84) or the Floating Pen (p. 87), or instead of a ruler in the Sticky Ruler (p. 92), and it plays an essential role in Magic Washing (p. 182) because without the wand the trick won't work!

However, the main use of a magic wand (and the real reason why so many magicians use it) is misdirection. Misdirection is one of the most important parts of a magician's job. It is the name magicians give to the art of making you look where they want you to look. Stage, television and film directors do the same thing by drawing your attention to the action.

Magicians call it misdirection because, as well as making sure you follow the plot (or "effect") of the trick (what is supposed to be happening) they have to keep your attention away from the secret (the "method") of the trick (what is really happening).

The magic wand can assist in this in several ways. For example, if you have something concealed in your right hand, you could pick up the wand with your left hand and wave it to make the magic happen. Without the wand, the audience may notice your suspiciously closed hand.

You can also use the wand to point. I know that everybody says that it is rude to point, but it is one of the most powerful ways of controlling the attention of your audience. If you point your wand – and, at the same time, look – at a particular prop on stage, everybody else will feel compelled to look at it, too!

It is this ability to control an audience's attention that makes the great magicians great. Perhaps there is a drama or theatre studies teacher at your school who you could talk to about ways of directing and misdirecting an audience's attention.

You see, a magic wand may only be a painted piece of wood, but it can be truly 'magical'!

THE MAGIC TABLE

Next time you are entertained by a magician, take a few moments to check out their table! Really good "magic tables" are hard to come by, and many magic dealers build and sell tables designed specifically for magicians.

These tables don't actually do anything magical (although there are some with secret traps and holes that do!); they are just good surfaces on which to display and perform magic.

It is a good idea for you to use the same

table for all your rehearsals and performances. It will put your mind at rest when you come to perform if you are already familiar with the height, surface, etc. of your table. There's nothing worse than having to perform on a rickety, unstable table that a well-meaning host or hostess has found for you!

You don't need to spend a lot of money on buying a table; there is probably something suitable in your home. A small round-topped table with a smart scarf draped over it makes an ideal surface on which to display your props during a stage performance.

If you are planning on performing at children's parties, you might want to make, or have made, something more stable and self-contained. A colourful box into which you can store and dispose of your props might be more suitable. Some of the illustrations might give you some ideas of suitable designs.

You could use a record album (LP) case or a large file box, which you could decorate with stars and other magical symbols. This you could place on any chair or table

or you could even put it on the floor. If you do the latter, you might have to choose tricks that do not need a surface and can be performed "in your hands" (although you could rest small props on the lid of the box). You might also find that it is easier to have a box in which to carry your props if you have to travel to your shows by public transport.

ANDY'S MAGIC SHOW!

MISER'S DREAM

This is one of the true classics of coin magic, performed by professional magicians all over the world. The magician plucks coins from the air and tips them into a container. In the finale, the magician"s hands produce a stream of gleaming coins caught in mid-air.

Requirements:

A SPECIAL FAKE COIN, ABOUT TWO DOZEN GENUINE COINS, A CONTAINER (E.G. A HAT, A LARGE TIN, A SMALL PLASTIC BUCKET) AND A SPECIAL HOLDER.

Secret preparation: The special coin is made by drilling a hole in a small metal disc that is the same size as the coins (a blank pet's name tag is ideal for this as it already has the hole in it). Run a small loop of thread through the hole so that it can be placed over your thumb (Fig. A).

The special holder is made from an old sock! This will hold

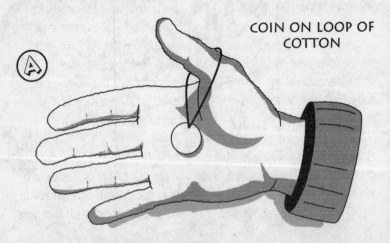

COIN ON LOOP OF COTTON

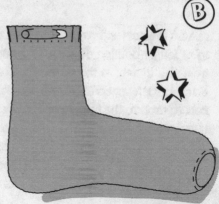

the stack of about a dozen coins that is necessary for your big finale. To make the holder, cut off the toe and sew elastic around the edge of the hole. Put the coins inside the sock – the elastic should prevent them falling out – and attach it with a safety pin under your jacket or coat on your right side (Fig. B).

Your final preparation is to loop the thread on the fake coin over your right thumb and stack the remaining coins (another dozen) in your closed left hand. The empty container should be on your table. All this set-up means that it is best to do Miser's Dream as an opening effect! It is particularly suited to this point in your show because of the noise, repetition of effect and short duration.

Pick up the container with the right hand and, keeping the special coin hidden in your hand, show the audience that it is empty. Pass the container to your left hand, while at the same time holding the coins inside it with the fingers and the inside top edge of the container.

Reach forward with the right hand, apparently to pluck a coin from the air. Keep the back of your fingers towards the audience, covering the fake coin dangling from your thumb. Jerk your hand upwards and this coin will flip up to your fingertips as if produced from mid-air.

Move the right hand to the top of the container and appear to drop the produced coin inside. What really happens is that you release the coin and it returns to its former position dangling from your thumb. At the same time, your left fingers allow one coin to drop to the bottom of the container, so that the audience can hear it. If the timing is right, this is very convincing.

By repeating the above steps, you can continue to produce coins from mid-air and drop them into the container! You can produce coins from behind your knee, from under your armpit or from your audience! It is very funny to seem to produce coins from behind spectator's ears, from their beards, etc.

When the last coin has been dropped from your left hand, allow your right hand to fall naturally to your side as you shake the container noisily and perhaps jokingly ask if anyone would like contribute to your collection! As the audience's attention is on the container, your right hand reaches under the right side of your jacket and squeezes the coins out of the holder. Any noise will be covered by you rattling the container in your left hand.

Finally, place the container on the table or the floor and open your right hand and let the final big production of coins stream from your hand into the container (Fig. C). The special coin will fall unnoticed among the real coins.

☆ TRICKS YOU CAN BUY

CASINO COIN

Magically you can change casino chips into real currency.

SHELL COIN

This special gimmicked coin will enable you to perform Coins Through The Table or Coins Across with ease.

COPPER SANDWICH

A more expensive gimmicked coin box which will enable you to perform more impressive effects.

TWENTIETH-CENTURY SILKS

Two handkerchiefs are tied together and set down to one side. A third silk handkerchief vanishes and reappears in an impossible place – tied in between the other two! The trick gets its name from the fact that it was considered ultra-modern when it was invented in 1890!

Requirements:

FOUR SILK HANDKERCHIEFS – TWO OF A MATCHING PLAIN COLOUR (LET'S ASSUME THAT THEY ARE RED) AND TWO MATCHING MULTI-COLOURED ONES. IT IS IMPORTANT THAT ONE CORNER OF EACH OF THE MULTI-COLOURED SILKS MATCHES THE PLAIN - COLOURED SILKS.

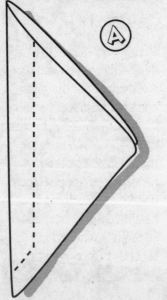

Secret preparation: One of the plain handkerchiefs has to be specially prepared by folding it in half and sewing the two halves together approximately 1 1/2 inches (4 cm) away from the folded edge. Use thread of the same colour as the silk so that the secret preparation will not be visible to the audience (Fig A).

Tie the corner of the prepared

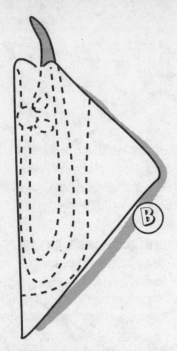

B

red silk to the corner of one of the multi-coloured silks, diagonally opposite its matching red corner. Push the multi-coloured silk into the secret pocket in the prepared handkerchief until only the red corner sticks out. It should appear that this is the corner of the red handkerchief (Fig B).

Display the two red silks and apparently tie them together. In fact, you are tying the corner of the genuine red handkerchief to the corner of the multi-

coloured silk hidden in the secret pocket (Fig.C). Then place the tied handkerchiefs somewhere on view: put them inside an empty glass or, for more fun, invite a member of the audience to hold them balled up between their hands.

That way, there is no way they can examine the handkerchiefs closely.

Make the duplicate multi-coloured silk handkerchief vanish by using one of the methods for vanishing a silk handkerchief that appear in this book.

Grab one corner of the two tied handkerchiefs and sharply pull them out of the glass, audience member's hands or wherever you chose to place them. This action pulls the hidden multi-coloured handkerchief from the secret pocket. The audience sees the handkerchief, which had apparently vanished just seconds before, now tied

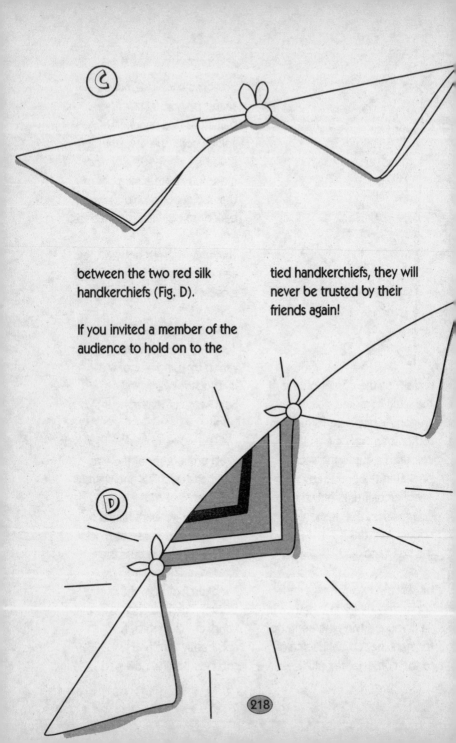

between the two red silk handkerchiefs (Fig. D).

If you invited a member of the audience to hold on to the tied handkerchiefs, they will never be trusted by their friends again!

THE COIN IN THE BALL OF WOOL

This is in the miracle class and, when well rehearsed, will make a great finale to any short act or show you are putting on. A borrowed coin is marked. It vanishes while held by a member of the audience and appears inside a sealed matchbox that was wrapped in the middle of a ball of wool!

Requirements:

A BALL OF HEAVY KNITTING WOOL, A POCKET-SIZED MATCHBOX, A LARGE CLEAR CONTAINER (BIG ENOUGH TO HOLD THE BALL OF WOOL), AND FOUR ELASTIC BANDS.

Secret preparation: You will also need a "coin vanishing handkerchief" made from any cotton handkerchief with a coin secretly sewn into one corner, and a special coin slide. The latter can be made from any piece of flat metal or

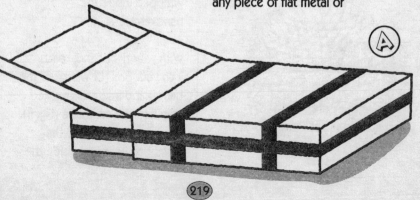

cardboard. This is folded into a flat tube so that a coin dropped into one end will slide down and out of the other end. This is the special secret gimmick for this effect.

Insert one end of the slide into the open drawer of the empty matchbox and wrap the four rubber bands around the matchbox. The bands will hold the slide in position and close the box when the slide is removed (Fig. A).

Wrap the wool around the matchbox to form a ball with the matchbox hidden inside. Make sure the wool is not wrapped too tightly otherwise the slide

(B)

may get stuck when you have to remove it at the crucial moment. Place the set-up ball of wool out of sight on your table. Inside a hat or large box is best.

Borrow a coin from any member of the audience and have them mark it with a pencil so that they will recognise it in the future. Wrap the marked coin in the special handkerchief. Underneath the cover of the handkerchief, you keep the borrowed coin "finger palmed" in your right hand and hand the secret sewn-in coin to a member of the audience to hold through the folds of the material. They will believe that they are holding the borrowed coin wrapped inside the handkerchief.

With your right hand, reach into your box (or wherever the ball is) and insert the marked coin into the coin slide (Fig. B). The coin will slide into the matchbox wrapped inside the ball of wool. After you have pulled the slide out of the ball of wool (and left the slide in the container), remove the ball of wool from the box and drop it into the clear container. Hand this to another member of the audience to hold.

Tell your "hanky-holding helper" to stand up and ask them if they are still holding on to the coin. After they have answered, whip the handkerchief out of their hand and display it on both sides to show that the coin has vanished.

Ask the spectator holding the ball of wool to stand up and face the audience. Hand the end of the wool to the spectator who lent you the coin and ask them to pull it. As they pull on the end, the ball of wool will twist and turn inside the container (Fig. C).

When the wool has all been unwrapped, the matchbox will remain inside the container. Ask another member of the audience to remove the box. Emphasize that at no point have you touched the box. Ask them to remove the rubber bands and open it.

Inside the drawer is the actual marked coin that vanished moments before! Return the coin to its owner for verification and take your bows.

SYMPATHETIC SILKS

Six large silk handkerchiefs behave in sympathy!

Requirements:

A LARGE ELASTIC BAND (MATCHING YOUR SKIN COLOUR), SIX LARGE SILK HANDKERCHIEFS OF CONTRASTING COLOURS, EACH APPROXIMATELY 30 INCHES (75 CM) SQUARE, AND A CHAIR.

Secret preparation: Tie three of the handkerchiefs together by the corners to form a chain (Fig. A). We will call these handkerchiefs A, B and C. Drape these handkerchiefs over the back of the chair so that

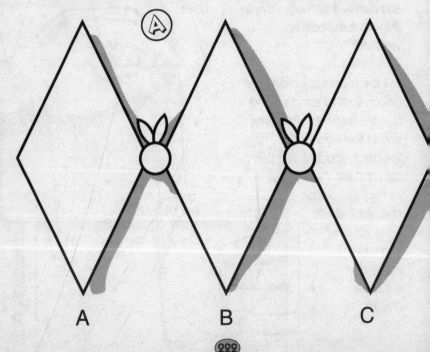

A   B   C

they appear unconnected. This is done by draping three untied corners over the front of the chair, with the knots hidden behind the back of the chair. Drape the three loose handkerchiefs (D, E and F) over the back of the chair alongside A, B and C (Fig B). Finally hook the elastic band over the little finger of your left hand.

Pick up D and hold its top corner between the thumb and index finger of your left hand. Pick up A, B and C together by the three untied corners and place these

corners between the left index and second fingers. The knots will remain hidden in the folds of the handkerchiefs. Finally E and F are

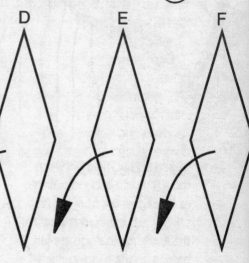

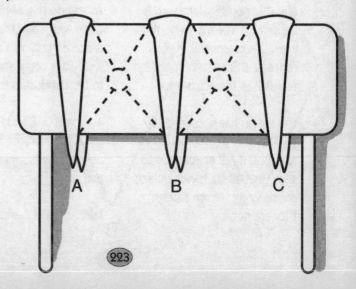

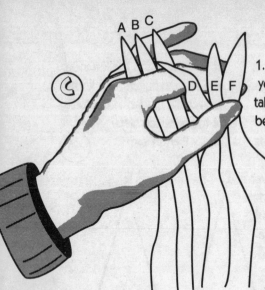

1. Hold both hands in front of you, and with the right hand take the first loose silk (F) from between the left thumb and index finger. Hold it up to the right, saying, "One."

2. Bring the right hand back to the left and remove silk E as you say, "Two."

3. Again bring both hands together, apparently to take another single silk, but what you actually do is replace E and F between the left thumb and index finger and take A, B and C between the right index and second finger. As you do this, say "Three." If done well – and this must be practised until you can do it well – this count should appear to be identical to the first two.

picked up and held between the left thumb and index finger, as far as possible from the first silk (Fig. C). It should appear to the audience that you are just picking up the handkerchiefs and that nothing untoward is happening. For this to be the case, it is essential that you rehearse this initial preparation as much as the actual trick.

This set-up has prepared you to do a special false count. This false count will enable you to show that all silk handkerchiefs are separate – even though they are not.

4. Count D, E and F from your left hand into your right hand, one at a time, saying "Four, five and six."

Take A, B and C and drop them

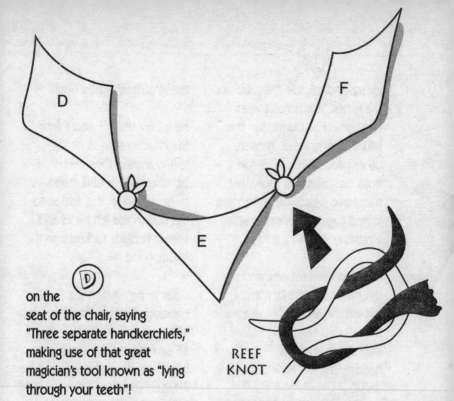

on the
seat of the chair, saying
"Three separate handkerchiefs,"
making use of that great
magician's tool known as "lying
through your teeth"!

Tie the corners of D,E and F
together with two reef knots
(right over left, left over right)
to form a chain of three (Fig.
D). Do not tie the knots too
tightly since, in a moment, you
will have to untie them
secretly! You do this by
apparently tightening the knots
by pulling on them. What you
actually do is shown in Fig. E.
This converts the reef knot into
a slip knot. Repeat this with
second knot.

REEF KNOT

Hold a knot in the palm of
each hand (Fig. F) and close
your hands around the knots.
As you do this, your fingers
hold on to the middle silk,
while the thumbs and index
fingers pull on the silks at

SLIPKNOT

either end to slide them free of the knots. You do all this as you appear to bundle up the silks into one hand. With the other hand, lift up A, B and C from the chair and show that they have miraculously become joined together, apparently in sympathy with D, E and F.

Place on the seat of the chair the now separate D, E and F (which the audience believes are still tied together) as you say, "Three knotted handkerchiefs." Now untie A, B and C.

As you are untying the knots, move the elastic band from around your left little finger and stretch it over all the fingers and thumb of the left hand. As each handkerchief is untied, tuck a corner inside the stretched elastic band.

Now pick up D, E and F from the chair to show that they, too, are untied. As each handkerchief in turn is shown to be separate, it is added to the silks in the left hand and a corner secretly tucked into the elastic band.

Offer to prove that the handkerchiefs are truly sympathetic silks. Throw them all into the air. It appears that, in mid-air, they all become knotted together. Of course it is really the elastic band holding them together and they were all connected before you threw them! This is a convincing illusion and a great ending to a classic piece of silken sorcery!

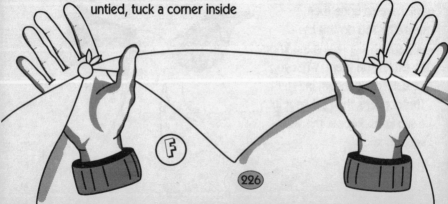

(F)

EGGS FROM NOWHERE

You produce an apparently endless supply of eggs from an empty handkerchief!

Requirements:

AN OPAQUE HANDKERCHIEF, A CONTAINER (E.G. A SMALL BASKET, A HAT), A PLASTIC EGG, A REAL EGG, A GLASS, SOME THREAD MATCHING THE COLOUR OF THE HANDKERCHIEF, AND A SUPPLY OF CONFETTI.

Secret preparation: Attach the plastic egg to one end of a 12 inch (30 cm) length of thread (the length will depend on the size of your handkerchief). Attach the other end of the thread to the middle of one edge of the handkerchief (Fig. A). (As an indication of the

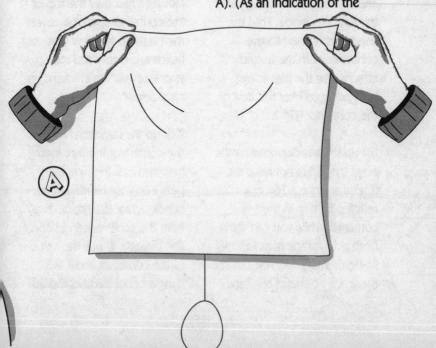

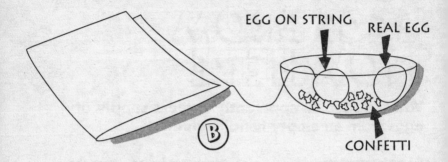

EGG ON STRING   REAL EGG

CONFETTI

B

thread's length, the egg should be hanging just below the middle of the handkerchief when the thread is attached to the hem.)

Fill the container with confetti and rest both the real egg and the fake egg inside. Fold the handkerchief next to the container, with the thread attached to the plastic egg being draped over the side of the container (Fig. B).

Lift up the handkerchief by the edge that does not have the thread attached. The egg remains hidden in the container while you can show both sides of the handkerchief to be ordinary. "As you can see there are no secret chickens

hidden in my handkerchief!" The audience will be wondering what you are talking about. They will soon discover . . .

Lay the threaded hem of the handkerchief over the top of the container so that it covers the plastic egg. Show that your hands are empty and roll up your sleeves. "No chickens up my sleeves!"

Pick up the handkerchief by the corners of the threaded hem and pull the hem tight between your hands. Lift the handkerchief straight up away from the container and table. The thread will pull the egg out of the container and it will dangle concealed behind the

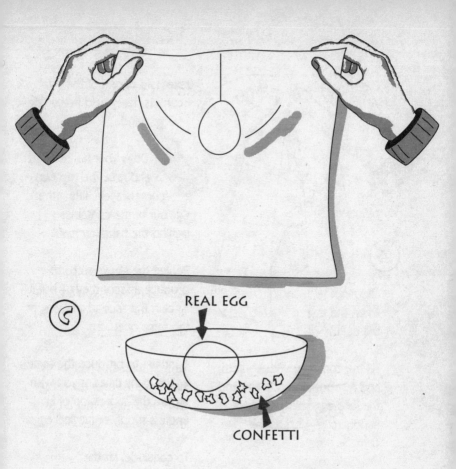

REAL EGG

CONFETTI

handkerchief (Fig. C).

Bring the top two corners together in your left hand, concealing the egg in the folds of the handkerchief (Fig. D). Your right hand holds the two lower corners together. The right hand with the corners moves up to the right until the folded handkerchief is held horizontally (Fig. E).

Move the handkerchief so that it is to the right of the container. Lift your right hand slightly and shake the egg out of the handkerchief. The egg will fall into the container and land on the confetti (Fig. F).

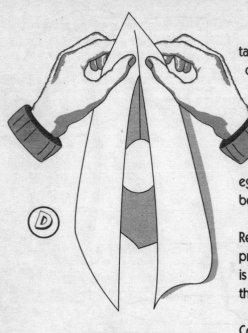

take hold of one of the two corners being held in the left hand.

Draw your hands apart and raise the top two corners again, lifting the egg out of the container behind the handkerchief.

Repeat the above steps to produce a second egg – but it is really the second showing of the same one!

Continue to produce the same egg as many times as you wish to give the impression of an endless supply of magical eggs.

To conclude, lift the handkerchief and egg out of the container for the last time and set them down on the table, ensuring that the egg is hidden inside the folds of the handkerchief.

Remove the real egg from the container and break it into the glass to prove that it is the real thing!

Now the audience will understand all this talk of invisible chickens!

Rest the handkerchief back on top of the container. The corners in the right hand go on the table in front of the container. The right hand moves up to the left hand to

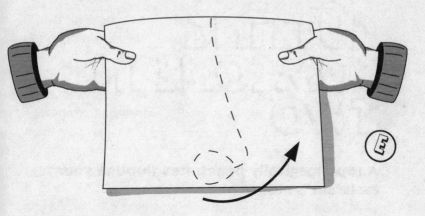

Finally pick up the container and walk towards the audience, who believe that it is full of real eggs. Make sure that they are unable to see into the container. Throw the contents towards the audience. They will be surprised – and pleased – to be showered only with confetti.

This makes a good finale to a show!

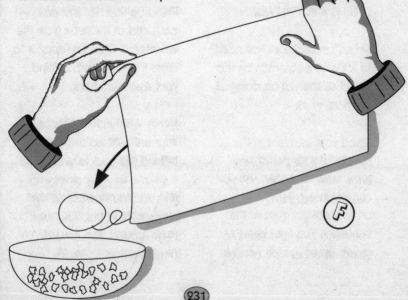

CUTTING SOMEONE IN TWO

A rope magically penetrates through your assistant"s stomach!

Requirements:

YOU ONLY NEED A LENGTH OF STRONG ROPE APPROXIMATELY 10 FEET (3 M) LONG AND A WILLING ASSISTANT. HERE WE'LL ASSUME THAT SHE'S A FEMALE, BUT A GIRL COULD HAVE A LOT OF FUN CUTTING A BOY IN TWO!

Secret preparation: You need to let your assistant in on the secret as she will be doing all the hard work.

Stand your assistant in the middle of your performing area. Make sure that nobody can see behind her.

You need two volunteers to stand on either side of your assistant. Ask each of them to hold on to an end of the rope and give it a good tug to show that it is a genuine rope. Your assistant stands behind the rope so that the halfway point passes in front of her stomach. Stand behind her and take each end of the rope from the volunteers. Then you appear to cross the rope ends behind your assistant's back.

Here's what actually happens. Your assistant holds her hands behind her back at waist level with one thumb pointing up (Fig. A). You don't cross the ropes behind her, you hook them around her upward-pointing thumb (Fig. B). Loop the right end over first, then the left end. Make sure the loops don't get twisted.

Cross the rope ends in front of your assistant and hand them back to the volunteers. Your assistant's thumb keeps the ropes taut. If she were to remove her thumb, the rope would just fall away.

Explain that you are going to cut your assistant in two in the same way that cheese is cut! Get the audience to join in by counting down before the volunteers pull on the rope. When you say, "Pull!" your assistant removes her thumb from the loops in the rope, and the rope appears to magically pass straight through her. Your audience can examine the rope – and your assistant – to their heart's content.

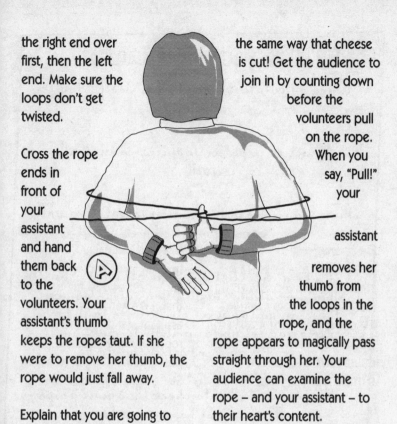

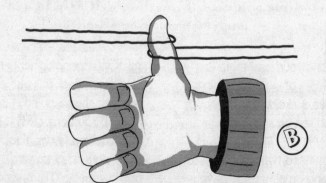

TOP TIPS FOR TRICKSTERS

When your talent "speaks for itself" don't interrupt

✧

Practice is perfection dressed in work clothes.

✧

There's no reward for having talent, that only comes from using it.

✧

Make a checklist of where all your props should be at the start of your act – on your table, in your pocket etc.. Refer to it each time you set up for a show to make sure everything is where it should be.

✧

It is a good idea to check that your props work okay just before you begin a performance, even if they worked fine the last time you used them. This will help to avoid any embarrassing situations!

✧

Don't worry if a trick goes wrong, most people realize and respect how hard magic is. If something goes wrong they will feel sympathetic towards you. The famous British magician Tommy Cooper was loved by audiences because his tricks went wrong!

WHAT NEXT?

Making all these tricks and learning them is fun, but at the end of the day, magic is about performing for other people – and that is even more fun. Okay, so you"ve shown your family and neighbours and a few friends and teachers at school, but what is the next step? It"s time to put together an "act" and put on a show . . . There is a big difference between being able to do a few tricks and putting on a complete act. This part of the book will help you to "get your act together" and find an audience to watch it!

WHAT IS AN ACT?

An act is the name people give to their performance. There are many different types of acts.

Stage acts:
These are performed on a platform or stage. You have probably seen these in theatres and on television. They often feature big illusions and require assistants.

Close-up acts:
Even when you are doing a few small tricks in situations where you only have a small audience and they are very close to you, it all works better if you have put the tricks together into a "routine". You can also put together in a more structured way a close-up act or show in which the audience sits around a table and watches. Close-up acts often feature tricks with coins and playing cards. You might have seen close-up

magic performed at your table in a restaurant or on television.

Patter acts:
As you know, patter is the name that magicians give to what they say when they perform, so you have probably guessed that patter acts are those in which the performer talks.

Silent acts:
Unlike patter acts, in a silent act the performer does not talk. In a silent act, the magic is performed to music and sometimes sound effects are used, too. You might have seen silent magicians on television, at the circus or in variety shows or pantomimes at the theatre.

Children's show:
This is an act or show devised specifically to entertain children. You might even remember seeing magicians entertain at school, on holiday or at parties.

TOP TIPS FOR TRICKSTERS

If you want to put a few tricks together to make a short act, remember that the opening trick should ideally be short but exciting and not involve anybody getting up from the audience to assist you.

☆

If you are putting together a routine or short act, try to intersperse short tricks between the longer more complicated routines (e.g. any effects involving a lot of dealing). This will provide more variety to your performance.

☆

Another good way to provide variety to your performance is by using different items as your props. For example, unless you are an expert it is probably not a good idea to do a long performance using only cards.

☆

Quieter moments in your performance are necessary to provide a contrast and will give the audience a chance to relax. This is a good time to invite members of the audience up to assist you.

WHAT KIND OF ACT DO YOU WANT TO DO?

The kind of act you decide to do will depend on your age and where you are able to perform. There is little point in deciding you want to do a David Copperfield-style big illusion show if you are only ten years old and your nearest theatre is 20 miles away!

When David was in his teens, he concentrated on performing sleight-of-hand close-up tricks and doing shows at birthday parties in the neighbourhood. The big spectacular illusions and glamorous assistants came much later!

You will probably find it easiest to start by putting on a show in your living room. If you know that only a few people are going to be there (say, under ten), you could make it a close-up show by setting up a big table and placing chairs around it. With a nice smart cloth on the table and a bright light pointing at the table top, even this can be made to look quite theatrical.

Or you could put together what used to be known as a "parlour show". This name comes from the days when families would entertain each other in the "parlour"! For this, you will need to clear an area for you to stand and perform and set out the chairs in a row so that everybody can see you. If there are any children, they could sit on the floor in a row at the front. Obviously you will need slightly bigger tricks than those you would use in a close-up show.

You could use the same show to entertain your friends in a classroom. Perhaps you could convince a teacher at school to let you perform your show for the class as a special treat?

Maybe you could transform your bedroom or living room into a small theatre and produce tickets, posters and programmes for your show! Do you have a brother, sister or friend who could sing, dance or juggle during an interlude in the show? You could make a small charge for the tickets and give any profits to charity.

Perhaps your school or an organisation that you belong to puts on special assemblies, concerts or shows during the year. When you feel confident, you could offer to perform a short magic

act for them. This will probably involve you performing on a stage – and that is a whole different experience!

You will need tricks that can be seen from the back of the audience. It's no good making a coin vanish for an audience of 200 – they wouldn't have been able to see it when it was there! You will need to hold up the props at around chest height so that everybody can see them clearly.

You might be faced with having to use a microphone. You will probably find it easier to keep it on a stand and hold the props in front of this. If you have to use a microphone, make sure that you have an opportunity to rehearse with it, so that you know exactly where it has to be to pick up your voice.

Of course, you could decide to do a silent act to music. This might be better if you do not enjoy speaking in public. If you are skilled in mime or dance (or would like to learn these skills), you might find a silent act a good way to communicate with your audience.

Whatever kind of act you want to do, you will find that joining a local theatre, drama or circus club or group will help to make you a better magician. And you'll probably find that they are keen to use your magical skills in many of their productions and shows. This is a great way to gain experience.

If you like and get on well with young children (4–8 year olds), you may find it worthwhile to put together a children's show that you can perform at birthday parties. Neighbours and friends are likely to snap up any offer for you to perform at their parties. You might even find that, after a while, parents are willing to pay you for it!

To hold the attention of an audience of young children requires great skill, which comes with experience. However, there are a number of pointers worth bearing in mind:

● Children like stories, so try to give some of your tricks a story-line patter.

● Children like bright colours, so make sure that your props and costume are vibrantly colourful.

● Children like to participate. You can invite one or two of them to assist you with a trick (tell them that only the well-behaved children can assist!) or get them all to help you by calling out a magic word or counting objects or shouting out colours.

● Children like to compete. You could break up your tricks by holding a funny competition, such as "Who can pull the funniest face?" or the Afghan Bands contest (p. 164).

COSTUME

What you wear when you perform will depend on the type of act you are going to do. Many magicians try to "theme" their acts around a certain style or character. Ali Bongo the Shreik of Araby is probably one of the best examples of a themed-character silent act. Ali uses a bright "Arabian Nights" costume when in character.

What suitable characters can you think of to perform magic? You could be a mysterious wizard in a long robe, or if you are doing a close-up show, you could be a croupier from a casino. With a friend playing the part of a teacher, you could wear a school uniform and do some of the items from the Classroom Tricks chapter of this book. If you are a girl, you could be a magical fairy! The possibilities are endless . . .

If you are not intending to play the part of a character and are just going to be yourself, dress as smartly as you can. However, it is also important that you feel comfortable and relaxed, so don't go overboard!

MORE TIPS FOR TALENTED TRICKSTERS

1. Magic with money is always more effective if the coins or banknotes used in the trick are borrowed from trustworthy members of the audience.

2. Tricks with coins are fine for showing a few people close around you (close-up magic), but – with a few exceptions (like Miser's Dream described in the Showtime chapter) – are not really suitable on stage.

3. If you perform coin productions on a stage or platform, it is worthwhile having the coins silver-plated so that they will shine in the stagelights and be easier to see.

4. If you are performing any tricks, remember that the audience's attention will be on your hands. Ensure that you give them a good wash before you perform!

5. Before you perform any tricks that will involve the audience concentrating on your hands, make sure that you have clean fingernails!

6. It is worthwhile washing your hands before and after you practise as props can become grubby and dirty very easily.

7. It is a good idea to keep your props especially for performing with. Keep these polished and clean to improve your "professional" image.

8. Many fake and gimmicked props are available from magic shops, dealers and suppliers. You may find a magic shop listed in your local Yellow Pages.

9. Gimmicked and fake props will enable you to do many more tricks - but it is essential to master the basics of sleight-of-hand magic first.

10. With a few well-practised tricks which you can perform with borrowed objects, you will always be able to entertain friends any time, any place, anywhere!

11. Money magic is not particularly suitable for an audience of young children as they may not be familiar with currency or its value.

12. Be warned! When people discover you are a magician many will say "If you're a magician produce some money then!" In this book you will find some tricks which mean that you can!

13. Even the most famous stage illusionists know a few small tricks that they can perform to maintain their reputation when off-stage!

14. You can have great fun with magic at any time. When out shopping you can produce the correct change from mid-air or vanish a note as you hand it to the bank cashier!

SUGGESTED SHOWS

CLOSE-UP SHOW

Jumping Band (p. 129)

The Haunted Key (p. 132)

Coin through Handkerchief (p. 140)

**Make Any National
Monument Vanish (p. 205)**

STAGE PATTER ACT

Miser's Dream (p. 212)

Torn and Restored Tissues (p. 156)

Just Chance (p. 62)

The Coin in the Ball of Wool (p. 219)

Cutting Someone in Two (p. 232)

Eggs from Nowhere (p. 227)

PARLOUR / CLASSROOM SHOW

With this show, you could talk about the fun you have at school being a magician.

The Professor's Nightmare (p. 175)

(You can talk about how you fooled your teacher by proving that three unequal ropes were equal!)

Doing Your Homework by Magic (p. 104)

(You can show how you do your homework by magic!)

Cut and Restored Skipping Rope (p. 145)

(How you helped a girl whose skipping rope had broken!)

Over the Teacher's Head (p. 114)

(And how some things are just over your teacher's head!)

STAGE SILENT ACT

Confetti-to-Candy Cup (p. 178)

Squared Circle Production Box (p. 180)

(To produce handkerchiefs for . . .)

Twentieth-Century Silks (p. 216)

(Produce more handkerchiefs and
ropes from the production box for . . .)

Magic Washing (p. 182)

(Use children from the audience. When
they return to their seats, give them
candy from the Confetti-to-Candy Cup
as prizes . . . and produce a giant load
of sweets from the Squared Circle
Production Box to end the act!)

CHILDREN'S SHOW

(To produce sweets or prizes for all the children)

SOME USEFUL ADDRESSES

CLUBS AND SOCIETIES

The Young Magicians Club,
  The Magic Circle Youth Initiative,
  Hertfordshire Business Centre,
    Alexander Road,
    London Colney,
      Herts. AL2 1JG,
      England.
(Membership open to 12- to 18-year-olds).

The Magic Circle,
  Chris Pratt,
    13 Calder Avenue,
      Brookman's Park,
        Herts, AL9 7AH.
        England.
(Open to those 18 years and older).

The Society of Young Magicians,
  Richard Blowers,
    P.O. Box 510260,
      St. Louis,
        MO 63151-0260,
        U.S.A.

More Useful Addresses

MAGIC DEALERS

Hank Lee's Magic Factory, P.O. Box 789, MEDFORD, MA 02155, U.S.A.

Stevens Magic Emporium, 2520 E. Douglas, Wichita, KS 67214, U.S.A.

Dynamix Fx Ltd.,Herts Business Centre, Alexander Road, London Colney, Herts. AL2 1JG, ENGLAND.

Kaytnar Magic Co., 189a St Mary's Lane, Upminster, Essex. RM14 3BU, ENGLAND.

MAGIC MAGAZINES

MAGIC
7380 S. Eastern Ave., Suite 124-179,
Las Vegas, NV 89123, U.S.A.

GENII
P.O. Box 36068, Los Angeles, CALIF 90036, U.S.A.

ABRACADABRA The World's Only Magical Weekly
Goodlife Publications Ltd., 150 New Road,
Bromsgrove, Worcs. B60 2LG, England.

THE YOUNG MAGICIAN
The Young Magicians Club, The Magic Circle Youth Initiative, Herts. Business Centre, Alexander Road, London Colney, Herts. AL2 1JG, England.